GLORY IN THE CHURCH

Colin Dye

Sovereign World

Sovereign World Ltd
PO Box 777
Tonbridge
Kent TN11 0ZS
England

Scriptural quotations are from the New King James Version, Thomas Nelson Inc., 1991.

ISBN 1 85240 204 0

This Sovereign World book is distributed in North America by Renew Books, a ministry of Gospel Light, Ventura, California, USA. For a free catalog of resources from Renew Books/Gospel Light, please contact your Christian supplier or call 1-800-4-GOSPEL.

Typeset by CRB Associates, Reepham, Norfolk
Printed in England by Clays Ltd, St Ives plc.

FOREWORD

The material in this *Sword of the Spirit* series has been developed over the past ten years at Kensington Temple in London as we have sought to train leaders for the hundreds of churches and groups we have established. Much of the material was initially prepared for the students who attend the International Bible Institute of London – which is based at our church.

Over the years, other churches and colleges have asked if they may use some of our material to help them establish training courses for leaders in their towns and countries. This series has been put together partly to meet this growing need, as churches everywhere seek to train large numbers of new leaders to serve the growth that God is giving.

The material has been constantly refined – by myself, by the students as they have responded, by my many associate pastors, and by the staff at the Bible Institute. In particular, my colleague Timothy Pain has been responsible for sharpening, developing and shaping my different courses and notes into this coherent series.

I hope that many people will use this series in association with our developing Satellite Bible School, but I also pray that churches around the world will use the books to train leaders.

We live at a time when increasing numbers of new churches are being started, and I am sure that we will see even more startling growth in the next few decades. It is vital that we re-examine the way we train and release leaders so that these new churches have the best possible biblical foundation. This series is our contribution to equipping tomorrow's leaders with the eternal truths that they need.

Colin Dye

CONTENTS

INTRODUCTION

There can be very few people who have not heard of 'the church', yet nearly everyone seems to have a different idea about it. Most ordinary people appear to think that the church is a building or denomination, and many believers assume that it is a series of meetings or services.

Even those of us who know that 'the church' is 'the people', who have heard about 'the body of Christ', often have very different ideas about how the church should be organised and what it should do.

Some leaders think that the church is all about worship, other ministers insist that evangelistic mission is what really matters, and a few clergy focus on caring for needy people in practical ways.

When we attend a variety of churches we soon find it hard to believe that they are all the same church of God. We discover that many leaders wear ceremonial robes, while others are casually dressed; that some clergy read their services from a book, while others seem to make it up as they go along; that most church services are over in forty minutes, but many last for several hours; that a few ministers still chant in seventeenth century English, while others sing in tongues. It can all seem terribly confusing.

Sadly, there is often considerable suspicion, even competition, between different churches in an area – or even within a denomination. Many believers realise that some genuine Christians must attend the other churches in their locality, but they cannot work out why!

If the church is important to God, we ought to try to understand the basic scriptural principles about the church so that at least we know what are matters of culture and taste, and what are matters of doctrine.

For example, it may not matter to Jesus whether we prefer service books or spontaneity, medieval chanting or modern choruses, robes or plain clothes. But it does matter to him when we separate ourselves from each other, when we refuse to engage in spiritual warfare, and when we quench the Spirit by our attitudes.

This book is for believers who will set aside their ideas about the church, and will study God's word to discover God's revelation about God's church. We need to know *his* vision and purpose for the church.

Please make sure that you read each scriptural reference – and tick the margin reference boxes as you go along to show that you have. Answer every question and think through each point as it is made. Before moving on to a new section, think carefully about the implications of what you have studied. Please allow God to speak to you about 'your' church as you study his word.

At the end of the book, there is some activity material. Please make sure that you study Parts 1–11 before beginning to work through the activities, as this will ensure that you have an overview of the biblical teaching about the church before you try to apply the details of any one area. These activities will help you to grasp and apply the scriptural material that you have studied.

You will also be able to use the activity pages when you teach the material to small groups. Please feel free to photocopy these pages and distribute them to any group you are leading. Although you should work through all the activities when you are studying on your own, please don't expect a small group to cover all the activity material. Instead, prayerfully select those parts that you think are most relevant for your group. This means that, at some meetings you might use all the material whilst at others you might use only a small part.

By the time you finish this book, it is my prayer that you will grasp that God has always wanted to reveal his glory in the church by Christ Jesus; that he is going to reveal his glory in the church so that all the nations of the world will come to the light; and that you will know how you can work in partnership with him to bring this about in your area.

Colin Dye

PART ONE

the glory of god

Many believers today do not expect to turn to the Old Testament when they study the church. They assume that the New Testament, especially the epistles, contains everything they need to know about God's plan for the church.

This approach, however, focuses too quickly on the small details and overlooks the larger picture. The church is an extremely significant part of God's purposes for humanity, but there is much that we will miss if we ignore the Old Testament foreshadowings of the church and the wider ways that God has dealt with his people through the generations.

For example, we will not understand the New Testament teaching about the church as 'God's building' without some knowledge of the Old Testament tabernacle and Temple; we will not grasp Paul's references to 'the bride' without some awareness of the Old Testament passages about 'the beloved'; and we will not appreciate the significance of the Lord's Supper without examining the Passover.

Most important of all, believers should try to understand the destiny of the church before they examine its detail. It is pointless, for example, to be able to define an apostle and list the duties of a deacon without grasping why God has given apostles and deacons to the church, and what their small place is in God's eternal scheme.

Put simply, every scrap of scriptural teaching about every aspect of the church is offered with the single aim of bringing glory to God and revealing his glory in and to the world – and to the principalities and powers in the heavenly places. If the main over-arching aim of the church – as seen in Ephesians 3:8–21 – is not perceived and remembered, it is all too easy to become unbalanced by over-emphasising some small aspect of church life and doctrine.

Ephesians 3:8–21 ☐

The purpose of God

The title of this volume in the *Sword of the Spirit* series is taken from Ephesians 3, where the climax of Paul's revelation about God's eternal purposes for humanity is his prayer for 'glory in the church'.

After reading Ephesians 3, we should be able to grasp that – throughout all ages, world without end – the out-shining of his glory, both on earth *and* in the heavenlies, is absolutely central to God's will. We also see that it is 'glory-in-the-church-by-Christ-Jesus'.

It is not possible, however, to appreciate the full significance of our Ephesians 3 destiny without some awareness of the Old Testament teaching about the glory of God.

Most evangelical and pentecostal believers know that the glory of God is one of the greatest themes in Scripture. In reflection of this, shouts of 'glory' are commonly heard during times of celebration, pleas for 'glory' are often made in fervent times of prayer, and the word itself features in many of our songs and hymns.

We want God to be glorified and we want to experience his glory. But some modern believers seem to forget that, in the Bible, glory is closely associated with sacrifice. We see, for example, that:

Exodus 24 ☐

- Exodus 24 reports that God's glory appeared to the seventy elders on Mount Sinai – after a sacrifice

Leviticus 9:6–24 ☐

- Leviticus 9:6–24 shows that God's glory was regularly seen in the wilderness tabernacle – at the hour of sacrifice

Exodus 40:29–35 ☐

- Exodus 40:29–35 describes the only way into the tabernacle – the altar of sacrifice

- 1 Kings 8:1–11 records that God's glory filled the Jerusalem Temple – after innumerable sacrifices had been made

- Hebrews 1:3 states that Jesus was always the outshining of God's glory – but John 7:39; 12:23–28; 13:31; 17:5 & Hebrews 2:9 show that his sacrificial death on the cross was the supreme revelation of God's glory

- Romans 8:18 teaches that we must share in the sufferings of Jesus' sacrifice – if we want to share in his glory

Glory is an onomatopoeic word; sacrifice is not. The sound of glory sounds great in our mouths, whereas the idea of sacrifice often grates in our throats. Both words are commonly misunderstood, but a right understanding of glory and sacrifice – and of the relationship between them – is vital if we are to appreciate the church's chief purpose and to set the small details of church life into their proper context.

GLORY

The Hebrew word for glory is *kabod*, which literally means 'heaviness' or 'weight'. This is occasionally used to describe the material prosperity, physical splendour or good reputation of a man or woman – for example, Esther 5:11 and Job 19:9. Less commonly, it poetically describes the warriors of a nation or the soul of a person.

But *kabod* is normally reserved for God. We see it, for example, in: Exodus 16:7; Numbers 14: 10, 21; Deuteronomy 5:24; 1 Kings 8:11; 2 Chronicles 7:1–3; Psalm 19:1; 113:4; Isaiah 35:2; 60:1–2; Ezekiel 10:4 & 43:2.

In the Old Testament, the expression ' the glory of God' is used in two different ways:

- *as a parallel term to 'the name of God' which refers to the self revealed character of God*

- *as a visible revelation of God's presence to his people*

This means that God's glory shows people – and principalities and powers – precisely where God is, and exactly what he is like.

1 Kings 8:1–11 ☐
Hebrews 1:3 ☐
John 7:39 ☐
        12:23–28 ☐
        13:31 ☐
        17:5 ☐
Hebrews 2:9 ☐
Romans 8:18 ☐

Esther 5:11 ☐
Job 19:9 ☐
Exodus 16:7 ☐
Numbers 14:10 ☐
        14:21 ☐
Deuteronomy
        5:24 ☐
1 Kings 8:11 ☐
2 Chronicles
        7:1–3 ☐
Psalm 19:1 ☐
        113:4 ☐
Isaiah 35:2 ☐
        60:1–2 ☐
Ezekiel 10:4 ☐
        43:2 ☐

In the New Testament, both these aspects of glory were perfectly fulfilled in Jesus. He was both the complete self-revelation of God's character and the clearest possible revelation of God's presence.

Today, it is the church's function both to show God's holy character to the world, and to be seen by the world – and by the powers in the heavenlies – as the place where God resides. This is why some knowledge of glory is basic to an accurate understanding of the church.

Doxa

Luke 9:32 ☐
John 2:11 ☐
    17:24 ☐
Romans 16:27 ☐
1 Corinthians
    11:7 ☐

The Greek word *doxa* is used in the New Testament for glory. Like *kabod*, this can refer to human honour; but it is normally used to describe a revelation – by grace and powerful deeds – of God's nature. We see this, for example, in Luke 9:32; John 2:11; 17:24; Romans 16:27; 1 Corinthians 11:7 & 2 Corinthians 4:4–6.

2 Corinthians
    4:4–6 ☐
John 2:1–12 ☐
    11:1–44 ☐

Doxa means everything that *kabod* does, and then adds to it a sense of a demonstration of beautiful perfection and a display of magnificent power. God's glory seen in Jesus shows the Father's splendid excellence and the full extent of his regal authority. And, of course, God's glory in the church today is meant to reveal exactly the same excellence and authority – but this is only possible 'by Christ Jesus'.

This glory was seen in John 2:1–12, when Jesus revealed God's grace and power by turning water into wine. It was visible in John 11:1–44, when Lazarus was dramatically resuscitated. And it shone at Jesus' transfiguration, resurrection and ascension.

But it was never so bright as at Calvary; for there – at the place of sacrifice – was seen the complete self-revelation of God's nature, the greatest possible demonstration of his grace and love, the supreme manifestation of his absolute holiness, and the perfect display of his beauty, power and authority.

Ephesians 3:21 ☐

When, today, believers sing or pray for God's glory to be seen, they are actually asking that the world will see God's holiness, grace and power. But these can only be seen 'in the church' – which is precisely why Paul pleads for 'glory in the church, by Christ Jesus, throughout all ages, world without end'.

Whenever we sing something like 'Glorify thy name', we are pleading for God's character, beauty and majesty to be unveiled to the world.

Yet these can be seen only in and through the church. If God's glory is not visible in the church, the world will never see it anywhere else.

Every time we cry 'glory', we encapsulate all that God is into one word – and should shake with awe, for this glory is our destiny.

The destiny of glory

1 Corinthians 11:7 shows that humanity was made as the image and glory of God: this means that, together, we were meant to be a complete revelation of God's nature and presence. Romans 3:23 reminds us that we have fallen very short of this glorious destiny.

1 Corinthians 11:7 ☐

Romans 3:23 ☐

Jesus, however, fulfilled the destiny and, by his sacrifice, made it possible for all humanity both to experience and to demonstrate the glory of God. This is made plain in Hebrews 2:6–10.

Hebrews 2:6–10 ☐

Jesus was glorified at the place of supreme sacrifice. It was there on the cross that he received a crown of great glory as the reward for his voluntary death. It was there, by his loving sacrifice, that he made it possible for us to see and reflect God's glory, and to begin to be transformed into God's likeness with ever-increasing glory. Because of the cross, God's glory seen in the face of Jesus Christ can now be seen in, and can be reflected by, the church.

The glory of God is the church's destiny. We were made to be a visible revelation of God's character and presence; we have fallen short of this, but the death of Christ has made it possible again. Glory is the church's birthright. The beauty and majesty and holy nature of God are held out to the church. But, in our rejoicing, we must remember that it is the glory of the cross: it is glory-in-and-through-sacrifice.

The yearning for glory

One of the great cries of the Old Testament prophets was that God's glory would one day fill or cover the earth. God himself promised this in Numbers 14:21 and Habakkuk 2:14.

Numbers 14:21 ☐

Habakkuk 2:14 ☐

Ezekiel 43:1–5 looks forward to that day, and 39:21–29 makes it clear that God's glory will affect *all* nations, not just the Jews. Significantly, both these passages also suggest that the Spirit will play a vital part in the revelation of God's glory to all nations.

Ezekiel 43:1–5 ☐

39:21–29 ☐

Isaiah
        59:21–66:24 ☐

Isaiah 59:21–66:24 looks forward to a time when all nations can see God's glory, and shows that the anointing of the Spirit is central to this revelation of God's grace, power and presence. (Significantly, this is one of only two Old Testament passages where the Spirit is identified as the Holy Spirit – the name by which he is known to the church.)

It is not difficult to recognise that Isaiah 60–66 is looking forward to the church – to the holy people, to the redeemed of the Lord, to those who have been sent to the nations to declare God's glory among the Gentiles. All the detailed New Testament teaching about mission, spreading the gospel, making disciples of all nations, reaching out to the Gentiles, and so on, is only the fulfilment of a plan whose outline shape can be seen in Old Testament chapters like these.

The central aim of God's great eternal plan has always been for his church to fill his world with his glory. He longs for us, together, to reveal his character and presence, to radiate his holiness and love, to display his authority, perfection and power. But we must not forget that the whole thrust of the Old Testament teaching about God's glory is that it is seen only – as at Calvary – where there is selfless sacrifice.

GLORY IN AND THROUGH SACRIFICE

Genesis 3:16–21 ☐

Sacrifice began with God. He made the first sacrifice. He spilt the first blood. He suffered the first loss. In Genesis 3:16–21, God himself slew, then skinned, some of the perfect creatures he had only just made.

This incident teaches much about sacrifice, but – for this book – its importance lies in its revelation that grace and love are the motives for godly sacrifice, not legalism or duty. In the Garden, God set the standard of high personal cost which was then followed by men and women as they offered him the best that they had in thanksgiving, praise, dedication, worship, adoration and commitment. We see this, for example, in Genesis 4:3–5; 8:20 – 9:17; 22:1–19 & Exodus 5:1–5.

Genesis 4:3–5 ☐
      8:20–9:17 ☐
      22:1–19 ☐

Exodus 5:1–5 ☐

Later, in the wilderness, God laid down the pattern of ritualistic blood sacrifices which his people faithfully followed for hundreds of years. These stressed God's gracious initiative and the people's absolute dependence on him.

Practical actions

As time went by, this system was abused – as grace so often is – and the realisation grew that the system was not final. The prophets began to plead for an extra type of sacrifice; for practical actions as well as symbolic gestures, for personal morality to be wedded to legal ritual.

Psalm 50:8–23; 51:16–19; Proverbs 15:8; 21:27; Isaiah 1:11–20; 58:1–14; 66:1–4, 18–21; Jeremiah 6:20; 7:21–28; Daniel 3:38–43; Hosea 8:11–13; Amos 5:21–24 & Micah 6:6–8 illustrate this critical development in the prophetic awareness of God's will. Most of the practical teaching in the New Testament about church life is rooted in prophetic passages like these.

The new understanding of sacrifice as both a ceremony pointing to our atonement in Christ and also a continuous holy way of life reached its Old Testament climax in the four songs of the servant of the Lord – Isaiah 42:1–9; 49:1–6; 50:4–11 & 52:13–53:12. These present a person whose death makes sacrificial atonement for others, and whose life is characterised by love, justice, humility, suffering and self-sacrifice.

These songs point to Jesus. In fact, all the Old Testament sacrifices prophetically point to him, for they express a need which only he fully satisfies, embody a faith which only he can justify, and demand a lifestyle which only he makes possible.

In the Old Testament, the victim slain may have been a substitute, but the worshippers always had to deny themselves in some way for God: they had to give him the best that they had. This needs to be remembered in the church today. Jesus may have died in our place to cover our sins, unite us with each other and bring us to God; but self-denial is still the 'ritual' demanded of the lives that he rules.

The secret of fruitfulness

Sacrifice is central to the teaching of Jesus. As soon as the disciples realised that he was the Christ, Jesus explained to them what this meant – Matthew 16:21; Mark 8:31–32 & Luke 9:22. When the disciples protested, Jesus rebuked them and told them that the divine demand for self-sacrifice applied to them too – Matthew 16:24; Mark 8:34 & Luke 9:23. When the twelve did not walk away, Jesus offered them, in Matthew 16:27 & Luke 9:26, a hint of glory. Within a few days, the Father dramatically underlined this at the transfiguration.

Psalm 50:8–23 ☐
51:16–19 ☐

Proverbs 15:8 ☐
21:27 ☐

Isaiah 1:11–20 ☐
58:1–14 ☐
66:1–4 ☐
66:18–21 ☐

Jeremiah 6:20 ☐
7:21–28 ☐

Daniel 3:38–43 ☐

Hosea 8:11–13 ☐

Amos 5:21–24 ☐

Micah 6:6–8 ☐

Isaiah 42:1–9 ☐
49:1–6 ☐
50:4–11 ☐
52:13– 53:12 ☐

Matthew 16:21–27 ☐

Mark 8:31–34 ☐

Luke 9:22–26 ☐

Matthew
        20:25–27 ☐

Luke 19:28–38 ☐

Mark 12:28–44 ☐

John 12:1–8 ☐
        13:1–16 ☐
        12:23–33 ☐

Genesis 4:3–5 ☐

Hebrews 11:4 ☐

As the time of Jesus' ultimate sacrifice drew near, he taught more clearly about self-sacrifice. We see this in Matthew 20:25–27; Mark 10:41–45; Luke 22:24–27; Matthew 21:1–11; Mark 11:1–11; Luke 19:28–38; John 12:12–16; Mark 12:28–34; Mark 12:41–44; Matthew 26:6–13; Mark 14:3–9; John 12:1–8 & 13:1–16.

Most important of all, in John 12:23–33, Jesus taught that self-sacrifice is the secret of fruitfulness. Before any seed can multiply, it must die and cease to be. If the seed seeks to preserve its own independent existence, it will remain a single grain; but when it dies and disappears, it yields a rich harvest. In John 12:23–33, Jesus applied this principle both to himself and to all who will follow him. Once again, we see how the Scriptures link glory with self-sacrifice.

Self-preservation leads to nothing except the preservation of self. Self-sacrifice leads to growth, glory and fruitfulness. Our calling in the church is to die to ourselves on behalf of others. This is the grace and love that God is seeking in his people – and a secret of church growth.

Faith was first linked to sacrifice in reference to Abel – Genesis 4:3–5 & Hebrews 11:4. Since then, it has always taken faith to offer God our 'self' as a sacrifice. But when we do risk everything by faith, we discover that the death of 'self' is never the end. The cross might be the universal symbol of the church, but the empty tomb is always before us. Godly, selfless self-sacrifices, which are motivated by grace and love, always lead to growth and glory in the church.

God will raise his church in this life to a wonderful new of loving. He will bless the church with his character and presence. He will use the church to show the world his holiness and love. He will reveal his authority, perfection and power through the church. God's glory will fill that tiny part of the earth where we are. There will be glory in the church for people of our nation to see.

The rest of this book is concerned with the New Testament teaching about the church – with the small details. In every section, however, please remember the big picture and appreciate that every detail has been given so that God's glory-in-the-church will be seen in all nations.

Many leaders disagree about different aspects of church doctrine and life. Whenever we are faced with such a dilemma, we must remind ourselves that God's glory is seen in sacrifice. The over-arching rule is plain: growth and glory stem from service and sacrifice. All our thinking about the church must be undergirded by this basic principle.

PART TWO

the church of christ

Every believer knows that the church is 'the church of Christ'. It belongs to him; it is 'his' church – which means that it can rarely be right for anyone to refer to 'my' or 'our' church.

Not all believers realise, however, that – strictly speaking – Jesus taught almost nothing about 'the church'. In fact, he mentioned it only twice in all his teaching – in Matthew 16:18 and 18:17. Of course, much of Jesus' teaching is directly relevant to the church, although it does not refer to the church by name.

Matthew 16:18 ☐
18:17 ☐

Matthew 16:18 is very well-known. It contains Jesus' famous promise to build his church on the rock-like foundation of Peter's profession that Jesus is the Christ, the Son of the living God – that the longed-for Messiah *and* the mighty miracle-working God were present in one person among them.

Some leaders think that Peter was the rock, rather than his profession; but the important point to grasp is that *Jesus* is the builder. In this passage, *he* promised to build *his* church – and to build it so strongly that the gates of Hades could not prevail against it.

We know that gates are defensive rather than offensive. No army attacks another one using the weapon of gates. Instead, an army which is under attack hides behind its gates, hoping that they will be strong enough to keep out its attackers.

This means Jesus is suggesting that his church will be essentially offensive. It will go to the gates of Hades to raid, perhaps to rescue those who are held captive. And the gates of Hades will not prevail; they will not be able to withstand the church's attack.

We have seen the Old Testament suggests that the church is meant to go to all nations, filling the earth with God's glory. And Matthew 16:18 shows that the church should be characterised by a warlike, offensive, nature. Taken together, we can expect that these ideas will be fundamental to the more-detailed teaching about the church in the rest of the New Testament.

CHRIST'S PRAYER FOR HIS CHURCH

John 17 ☐

Jesus' prayer for his disciples in John 17 reveals the longings in his heart just before his death and offers an outstanding picture of the church's purpose on earth. Once again, this is a broad picture which provides us with a panoramic view of God's purposes. The details of church life and doctrine that we will examine later should be considered in this 'over-all' context rather than studied in isolation.

Although John 17 does not specifically refer to 'the church', hindsight – plus a knowledge of the Old Testament passages we have read – makes it plain that this is Jesus' intercession for his church. In the prayer, Jesus begs for the church to be marked by five main characteristics:

- *the glory of God*

- *the Word of God*

- *the joy of God*

- *unity in the love of God*

- *sent into the world by God*

Revealing the glory of God

It should not surprise us that glory is the main burden of Christ's prayer, and he mentions 'glory' or 'glorify' eight times – verses 1, 4, 5, 10, 22 & 24.

Jesus prays that God will reveal himself so that his beauty, majesty, authority and holiness are clearly present in and among the church. We know that, in New Testament days, God revealed himself in Jesus: John 1:14 demonstrates this. Of course, not everyone recognised the glory of God in Jesus, and even those who did – as at the transfiguration – were not sure what to do about it.

We also know that, today, the glory of God is meant to be 'in the church'. Romans 8:21 is often translated as 'the glorious liberty of the children of God', but a more accurate rendering is 'the liberty of glory of the children of God'. This refers to the release or freedom we experience when God's glory is revealed among us, and this is what Christ is praying for in John 17:24.

Romans 8:21 ☐

As with Jesus in his day, not everyone will recognise God's glory when it occurs today, and – as at the transfiguration – some who do will not know how to respond. But we must never forget that there is meant to be glory in the church by Christ Jesus, and that it is meant to bring unity to the church, 17:22, and revelation to the world, 17:23.

This stress on glory has four serious implications for the church today. It means that:

- *the world's understanding of God depends on what it sees of him, and of his attitudes and activities, in the church*

- *the glory of God is manifested in human form; it is not a ghostly glow or a medieval halo, it is a practical dynamic which is seen in the lives of believers as they worship, work and serve together*

- *there must be an ongoing experience of the cross in the self-life of every church member individually, and in-and-between every congregation corporately – as 2 Corinthians 4:7–12 makes clear*

2 Corinthians 4:7–12 ☐

- *unity within the church and mission to the world are fundamental to Christ's purposes for us; they are not alternate emphases to choose between, rather they are the inseparable results of the presence of God's glory*

Some leaders suggest that the church should focus on unity, and that this will bring glory to God. Others insist that mission must be our priority, and that this will glorify God. In John 17, however, Jesus prays the reverse. He suggests that we should concentrate on knowing God's glory – and that this will bring about unity-and-mission.

This does not mean that a stress on mission and unity is wrong, merely that any such emphasis must be a loving, gracious, self-sacrificing response to a vital experience of God's presence, beauty, majesty and power. This is why, historically, the cross has always been central in every facet of church life, worship, service and architecture.

Guided by the Word of God

Jesus prayed about the Word and words of God in John 17, referring to them five times, in verses 6, 8, 14, 17 & 20. Jesus' prayer shows that he wants the Word to be central to the church. God's words, not human ideas or traditions, should determine every aspect of church life. John 17 suggests five things about the Word and the church:

1.   *the church guards the Word of God*

Verse 6 suggests that the church must 'keep' the Word. The Greek verb here, *tereo*, means 'guard' or 'keep safe' rather than 'obey'. This shows that the church has a special responsibility to keep God's word safe and to ensure that nobody tampers with it, changes it, adds to it, or takes anything away from it.

This does not mean that we are devoted to a particular translation of the Bible and a simplistic interpretation of every verse. Instead, it means that we must work hard at understanding the historical, cultural and religious settings in which the Word was given so that we can relate to it accurately today.

2.   *the church listens to all the words of God*

Verse 14 shows that 'the Word of God' is not restricted to the written Scriptures, but also includes the prophetically inspired words of God. Jesus did not encourage the church to be devoted only to the Old Testament, but also to all the words of God which Jesus 'gives'.

The church must listen very carefully to the Holy Spirit to discern what words of God Jesus is giving today. These will always be in accordance with scripture, but they will highlight certain aspects of the total truth of God's word which are particularly relevant for our situation – and these will probably be different from what was particularly relevant in the recent past.

3. *the church is sanctified by the Word of God*

Verse 17 states that the Word of God has a sanctifying function. The Greek verb, *hagiazo*, means to separate, and we examine this in Part Six of *Knowing the Spirit* in this *Sword of the Spirit* series.

As the church allows itself to be controlled, guided and directed by God's word, so the church becomes ever more separated from worldly thinking and attitudes, and even more committed to God and to his attitudes and actions.

4. *the Word is the whole truth*

Verses 17 and 19 show that God's word is 'the truth'. The Greek word here is *aletheia* which means the reality at the basis of everything. It does not refer only to a particular, objective, ethical truth, but to truth in all its fullness and scope.

This means that God's word is not just 'true', but that it is 'the whole truth'. It is not one truth amongst many truths; it is *the* truth besides which there is no other truth.

5. *the Word is vital for the church's mission*

Verse 20 reveals that God's word has a vital role in bringing people to belief in Jesus. The Word is not only to be guarded, studied, revered and used in teaching, it is part of the church's mission.

As it is God's word which brings people to belief in Jesus, we must ensure that his word is central to our mission. Again, this does not mean that we must only use direct quotes from a particular translation of the Scriptures; it means being guided by Jesus, through the Spirit, and passing on the words that he gives for the person or situation.

Filled with the joy of God

In verse 13 of his prayer, Jesus asked that his joy would be fulfilled in his disciples. He did not pray that *they* would be joyful, or that *their*

John 15:11 ☐
    16:24 ☐
    3:29 ☐

Acts 8:8 ☐
    13:52 ☐
    15:3 ☐

Romans 15:13 ☐

2 Corinthians 8:2 ☐

Philippians 1:4 ☐
    1:25 ☐

1 Thessalonians
    1:6 ☐
    3:9 ☐

2 Timothy 1:4 ☐

Hebrews 13:17 ☐

1 Peter 1:8 ☐

1 John 1:4 ☐

2 John 12 ☐

3 John 4 ☐

Isaiah 60:5–7 ☐
    61:3–7 ☐
    61:10–11 ☐

John 1:1 ☐
    8:24 ☐
    8:28 ☐
    10:38 ☐
    14:9–11 ☐

joy would increase; instead, he prayed that they would be fully filled – or completed – with *his* joy.

Jesus had often said this before – as in John 15:11 & 16:24; and John the Baptist had testified, in John 3:29, that his joy had been fulfilled because he had heard 'the bridegroom's' voice.

The Greek word for 'joy', *chara*, is closely related to the Greek word for 'grace', *charis*. Delight is the common factor in joy and grace; and joy, in the New Testament, is the natural human response to God's grace. We can say that God delights to give – that is grace – and that we are delighted – or joyful – when we receive his grace.

As the church exists only though and by God's grace, it is to be expected that we should be characterised by joy. We see that the New Testament church was filled with God's joy in, for example, Acts 8:8; 13:52; 15:3; Romans 15:13; 2 Corinthians 8:2; Philippians 1:4, 25; 1 Thessalonians 1:6; 3:9; 2 Timothy 1:4; Hebrews 13:17; 1 Peter 1:8; 1 John 1:4; 2 John 12 & 3 John 4.

We have seen that Isaiah 60–66 looks forward to the church, and 60:5; 61:3 & 61:7 teach that everlasting joy will fill the hearts of God's people. 60:7 and 61:3 relate this joy to God's glory; and 61:10–11 proves conclusively that joy is a consequence of grace. (We can consider Isaiah 61:10–11 to be one of the clearest Old Testament pictures of the church, pointing as it does to joy, grace, salvation, sanctification, the bride, and revelation to 'all the nations'.)

United in the love of God

In John 17, Jesus prayed four times that his disciples might be perfectly united in God's love – in verses 11, 21 & 23. The Greek word here is *hen*, which means 'one'. This shows that Christ is asking for 'oneness' – for union rather than unity.

Jesus prays that we will be 'one like us'. This means that the model for oneness is the relationship between the Father and the Son which Jesus describes in John 1:1; 8:24, 28; 10:38; 14:9–11 and 17:21–23.

Most church leaders stress different aspects of the oneness for which Jesus prays. They emphasise, for example, that:

- *the oneness of God means that churches should unite with each other in every possible way*

- *the triune diversity of God means that our unity must allow for denominational and traditional distinctions*

- *the intended evangelistic impact of the oneness means that our unity should be expressed in a common purpose in mission*

- *Jesus' prayer is a request for all believers to work together harmoniously*

- *John 14:11–12 means that our unity should be manifested in miraculous powers*

John 14:11–12 ☐

When taken together, these emphases are true and helpful. They have one weakness, however, for they all place the responsibility for oneness on our human shoulders. The fact that Jesus prays to the Father must presuppose that the church's oneness originates in divine action rather than in human endeavour. 17:22 shows that oneness flows from the Father, to the Son, to believers.

Most leaders seem to believe that oneness is a mystical union which will be fully seen only after the return of Jesus, but this is unacceptable. Verse 23 says 'they may be made perfect in one'.

The Greek verb is *teleioo* which means that the oneness is absolute, that it is perfected or completed. The verb is in the passive form, which means that believers are to be made one rather than that they are to make themselves one. And the time-scale is temporal rather than eternal. This oneness is not something which is reserved for heaven; it is for now so that our world may be effectively challenged about Jesus.

We will see later that this organic oneness is basic to most of the pictures of the church, for example, 'body', 'building', 'temple', 'bride' and 'vine'. But, for now, we simply need to recognise that the church should be characterised by unity and that our unity should be:

- *visible enough to challenge the world to believe in Jesus*

- *founded in God*

- *forged by God*

Jesus' prayer concludes his last supper teaching which includes, in 13:34–35 and 15:12–17, the theme of visible, sacrificial love for one another. In 13:35, the result of this love is very similar to the desired result of Jesus' intercession for oneness in 17:21–23. At the very least, this suggests a relationship between sacrificial love and oneness.

John 13:34–35 ☐
15:12–17 ☐

Sent into the world by God

Everything we have seen about the church suggests that going to all the nations of the world is central to the church's purpose. This is underlined in Jesus' intercession.

Jesus mentions 'the world' nineteen times in the prayer, and shows that the church:

- *is sent into the world* – in the same physical way that Jesus was sent into the world by the Father. The church has been commissioned to go into the world like Jesus, to live in the world like Jesus, and to challenge the world like Jesus.

- *is in the world but not of the world.* The church is called to be deeply involved in the world and to be integrated with the world, yet to be quite distinct from the world and unaffected by it.

- *is hated by the world.* The church will not be loved and applauded by the world when it loves with the love of God; it will be hated and bitterly persecuted. We examine this opposition in Part Four of *The Rule of God* in this *Sword of the Spirit* series.

- *is kept by God from the evil one. The same Greek word for 'to keep', tereo,* is used in verses 6, 11, 12 & 15. This means that the church is guarded by the Father; we are protected when the evil one attacks us, we are not given immunity from all his attacks.

We have seen that Matthew 16:18 suggests the church will be essentially offensive, and that the gates of Hades will not be able to withstand the church's attack. As the John 17:15 promise of protection is set in the context of going into the world with God's word and love, we should be able to grasp that it is expressing in different words the same truth as Matthew 16:18.

Throughout the Bible, God's word relentlessly emphasises that the church is meant to go to all nations and to fill the world with God's glory. In John 17, Jesus makes it transparently clear that the church really has been sent into the world so that the world will believe and so that God's glory will be seen. If we are not a mission-centred church, we are not really functioning as *his* church.

This foundation principle must be held continually in mind when we examine the more detailed New Testament teaching about the doctrine, structure, life and purpose of the church.

PART THREE

the gathering

The English word 'church' has many popular meanings. In a dictionary, it is usually defined as 'a place for public Christian worship', and most ordinary people automatically think of a building when they hear the word 'church'.

Other people confuse the word 'church' with Christian meetings. They ask, 'Are you going to church tomorrow?' when they really mean, 'Are you going to the meeting or service?'

Some believers associate 'church' with a particular denomination. They enquire, 'Which church do you belong to? Anglican, Baptist, Pentecostal, Assemblies of God...?' And a few people think of 'church' as the professional 'ordained' ministry and speak about someone 'going into the church'.

The English word 'church' comes from the Byzantine word *kurike* which means 'belonging to the Lord'; but the Greek word *ekklesia* is the New Testament word, and this literally means 'called out'.

Ekklesia is derived from the two Greek words *ek*, 'out of', and *klesis*, 'a calling'. This should make us think of Jesus' name for the Holy Spirit. Five times in John 13–17, Jesus referred to the Spirit as

John 14:16 ☐
14:25–27 ☐
15:26 ☐
16:7–11 ☐
16:14–15 ☐

the *Parakletos*, which means 'called alongside'. Somehow, the sense of 'God calling' is central to both the Spirit and the church – and so to our life in the Spirit and our life in the church. We examine the relationship between the Spirit and the church later.

EKKLESIA

Acts 20:28 ☐

1 Corinthians
    1:2 ☐
    11:22 ☐
    15:9 ☐

2 Corinthians 1:1 ☐

Galatians 1:13 ☐

1 Thessalonians
    2:14 ☐

1 Timothy 3:15 ☐

Matthew 16:18 ☐

The Greek word *ekklesia* is used in the New Testament over one hundred times, and is most commonly identified as 'the church of God'. We see this in Acts 20:28; 1 Corinthians 1:2; 11:22; 15:9; 2 Corinthians 1:1; Galatians 1:13; 1 Thessalonians 2:14 & 1 Timothy 3:15. This shows that the church has been called by God, that it belongs to him, that it is his church.

Greek background

When Jesus spoke about 'building his *ekklesia*' in Matthew 16:18, he was not inventing a new word which was meaningless to his disciples. He was using an everyday word which they fully understood, and was claiming that word to himself. If we are to understand correctly the New Testament teaching about the church, we must first appreciate what the word *ekklesia* meant at that time.

In Greece, the *ekklesia* was the electorate of a city. A herald summoned all the free men of the city to the council where they would debate and vote. This gathering was 'the assembly' or *ekklesia*.

We have seen that *ekklesia* literally means 'called out', and this refers to the calling by the herald of the citizens. At that time, however, *ekklesia* was taken to mean 'the gathering' or 'assembly' which was the result of the herald's summons.

Today, we come closest to the original meaning of *ekklesia* when we think of the church as 'the gathering of God'. We have been called out of the world to be gathered together in a relationship with Christ.

In Greece, every city *ekklesia* had unlimited powers. It elected and dismissed magistrates, generals and other military leaders. It was responsible for the conduct of all military operations. It raised and allocated funds to support its campaigns. It declared war and made peace. It assigned troops to different tasks and sent them from the city to fight on behalf of the city.

With this contemporary background, Matthew 16:18 becomes even clearer. It is plain that Jesus' *ekklesia* will behave like all the other ones: it will be essentially militant in character. If we do not grasp this elementary principle, we will misunderstand much of the New Testament teaching about the church.

Interestingly, every meeting of each Greek *ekklesia* commenced with prayer and sacrifice, and all free citizens had equal rights and equal duties. No one member was considered to be more important than any other. This is the picture which was adopted by Jesus for his gathering, his church; and we should therefore expect to find similar principles in the church which is governed by God.

Old Testament background

In the Greek version of the Old Testament, the Septuagint, *ekklesia* was used as the word for 'the congregation' of Israel. *Ekklesia* was used to translate the Hebrew word *qahal* – which comes from the verb 'to summon'. *Qahal* literally means 'an assembly called together'.

Israel was the redeemed people of God who had been delivered from slavery and summoned from Egypt to be ruled by God in the land of promise. Their redemption was the basis of their gathering together.

Unfortunately, most English translations of the Bible render both *qahal* and another Hebrew word, *edah*, as 'congregation'. *Qahal*, however, refers to 'the people' who have been gathered together, whereas *edah* refers to 'the event'.

Qahal appears almost 130 times in the Old Testament and is usually translated into English in one of three different ways:

- *congregation* – for example, Leviticus 16:17, 33; Numbers 10:7; 20:10; 1 Kings 8:14; 1 Chronicles 29:20; 2 Chronicles 6:3; Ezra 2:64; Psalm 22:22 & Joel 2:16

- *assembly* – Genesis 49:6; Exodus 12:6; Numbers 14:5; Deuteronomy 5:22; Judges 20:2; Jeremiah 50:9

- *company* – Genesis 35:11; Numbers 22:4; Jeremiah 31:8

Leviticus 16:17 ☐
16:33 ☐

Numbers 10:7 ☐
20:10 ☐

1 Kings 8:14 ☐

1 Chronicles
29:20 ☐

2 Chronicles 6:3 ☐

Ezra 2:64 ☐

Psalm 22:22 ☐

Joel 2:16 ☐

Genesis 49:6 ☐

Exodus 12:6 ☐

Numbers 14:5 ☐

Deuteronomy
5:22 ☐

Judges 20:2 ☐

Jeremiah 50:9 ☐

Genesis 35:11 ☐

Numbers 22:4 ☐

Jeremiah 31:8 ☐

It says much about the English translators' understanding of the church that they would not render *qahal* in only one way. Instead they translated it by context: if the setting was worship, they translated it as 'congregation'; if administrative, they called it 'assembly'; and if military, they called it 'company'.

But it is the same word and the same people of God. They had been gathered to God to praise, to organise themselves *and* to fight. Somehow we need to incorporate all the biblical meanings of *ekklesia* and *qahal* into our basic understanding of the church.

Acts 7:38 □

Acts 7:38 refers to Israel as 'the church in the wilderness', and we can see now that this was not picture language but an accurate description of God's gathered people. We consider the relationship between Israel and the church in Part Six; but, for now, we can learn four truths about God's church from the Old Testament 'church'.

1.   Gathered from the world

Hosea 11:1–12 □

Hosea 11:1–12 famously describes Israel as loved and called from Egypt. God called to the people of Israel and gathered them from Egypt into the promised land.

- *they were redeemed from slavery in Egypt*

- *they passed through the waters of the Red Sea*

- *they endured trials and temptations in the wilderness*

- *they defeated their enemies*

- *they entered Canaan*

All this foreshadowed the church's spiritual gathering from slavery to sin – through redemption, baptism, strengthening and spiritual warfare – to our promised inheritance and glorious destiny.

We know that Israel's 'salvation' was completely due to God's sovereign intervention: it was his work of grace. They could not free themselves from slavery; they could not cross the Red Sea or defeat Pharaoh's armies in their own strength; they could not survive in the wilderness without God's guidance and provision – and so on.

It is exactly the same for the church. We are God's gathering. He loves us and has called us from the world. He has gathered us to himself by a massive work of grace. Without his love, his sovereign intervention, his salvation, his strength, his guidance and his provision, there would be no church.

This means that we can expect the New Testament teaching about the church to emphasise these ideas of calling, grace and total dependence on God.

2.   Gathered together

Israel was called by God to be a community, a nation. The sons and daughters of Abraham were gathered together and their experience of God was essentially corporate.

- *they left Egypt together*

- *they went through the Red Sea together*

- *they ate and drank together* – 1 Corinthians 10:4

- *they crossed the wilderness together*

- *they faced their enemies together*

- *they experienced God together*

- *they entered Canaan together*

1 Corinthians
10:4 ☐

It is the same with the church. God's call is not only a private matter, and salvation is not just a personal affair. We are brothers and sisters in Christ. We are a new nation, a body, a building, and so on. The New Testament letters were written to groups of people who had been gathered together in particular localities. Without this strong community dynamic, a gathered church is meaningless.

This means we can anticipate that the New Testament teaching about the church will emphasise loving relationships, unity, practical caring, forgiveness and mutual acceptance.

3.   Gathered for a relationship

The people of Israel was not just gathered together aimlessly, they were called together so that they could enjoy a relationship with God. They were called to be *his* children, *his* people, *his* nation.

Genesis 17:1–8 ☐

Exodus 6:2–8 ☐

God's covenants with Abraham and Moses in Genesis 17 and Exodus 6 were the basis of this relationship. In both these passages God promised to take Israel as his people and to be their God.

God promised to live among them, and we see this in the pillar of fire, the tabernacle and the Temple.

It is the same with the church. Jesus is Emmanuel, 'God with us'. The Holy Spirit has been called alongside us to be with us. Our personal and corporate relationship with God is the foundation for everything.

Mark 3:13 ☐

When Jesus first 'called' the twelve disciples, Mark 3:13 shows it was so they could 'be with him'. They were called together into a relationship with Jesus, and their 'sending out' to deal with the enemy stemmed from this relationship.

This means that we can expect the New Testament teaching about the church to stress the priority of our relationship with God, to emphasis concerns like gathering together for prayer, worship, praise and fellowship.

4.   Gathered to a destiny

The calling of Abraham, in Genesis 17:1–8, involved a promise, a purpose, an inheritance, and a destiny. This is set out in Hebrews 11:8. The people of God were called to make a journey towards a clearly defined destination – the promised land of Canaan.

Hebrews 11:8 ☐

It is the same with the church. We have been gathered from our 'Egypt' for a journey towards our promised inheritance – there is a glimpse of this in 1 Timothy 6:12. We are heirs of God, joint-heirs with Christ, and we have received the Holy Spirit as the guarantee of our eternal destiny.

1 Timothy 6:12 ☐

We know that the church has been gathered together for a 'glorious' purpose. And we must begin to see ourselves as we truly are – gathered together in the stream of God's eternal plan. God is calling to himself one people, drawn from every nation, whose destiny is glory. And we are part of this.

In some amazing way that we neither understand nor appreciate, we are joined through the cross to countless millions of believers in every country and continent right across the world. And we are united with vast multitudes of brothers and sisters who are gathered round the throne of the lamb of God, with those believers who are already dwelling in his glory in his heavenly kingdom.

We are inexorably being drawn by God towards a wonderful final destiny which is set out in Ephesians 4:13. Just as the children of Israel knew that they would reach the promised Land, so too the church *will* come to the unity of the faith. We *will* reach the knowledge of the Son of God. We *will* form the perfect Man. We *will* be fully mature with the fullness of Christ. We *will* be filled with the utter fullness of God. We *will* be united with all things in heaven and on earth under one head, even Jesus Christ.

Ephesians 4:13 ☐

EXPRESSIONS OF *EKKLESIA*

We have seen that, by the time of the New Testament, *ekklesia* was a familiar term for God's people. It suggested the idea that God was preparing a people who would bring him glory and through whom he could show his love, grace and power to all nations.

The New Testament, however, does not use *ekklesia* to describe the church in only one way. Instead, *ekklesia* is used to present the church in three different, yet complementary ways.

Through *ekklesia*, we are introduced to the concepts of:

- *the universal church*

- *local churches*

- *household churches*

Each of these ways of expressing *ekklesia* is valid on its own. A more complete understanding of the church, however, can be achieved only by grasping all three expressions.

The universal church

This consists of all genuine Christians everywhere – on earth and in heaven. It is the entire company of believers, both living and dead.

This means that no church gathering or denominational grouping on earth can rightly be considered the universal church. It is invisible and has no expression of its own. Instead it is expressed on earth through *all* local and *all* household churches.

The universal church is referred to, for example, in Ephesians 1:22; 3:10, 21; 5:23–27, 32; 1 Corinthians 10:32; 12:28; Philippians 3:6; Colossians 1:18, 24 and 1 Timothy 3:15.

Local churches

In the New Testament, *ekklesia* is also used to identify all the believers in a locality – like a town, city or rural area. We see this, for example, in Acts 13:1; Romans 16:1; 1 Corinthians 1:2; 16:19; Galatians 1:2; 1 Thessalonians 1:1; Colossians 4:16 and Revelation 2:1–3:22.

It is important we recognise that a New Testament local church does *not* correspond with what is commonly called a local church today.

Modern local churches are usually smaller units of *ekklesia* than the church of an urban or rural region. Sadly, they often function independently of most other churches in their locality. This was not so in the New Testament, when all the churches in a region joined and co-operated together as the church in that locality.

For example, when Paul wrote to the church in Corinth, it was not to a small community assembly which was tucked away in a side street serving a tiny area. He wrote to a vast metropolitan church which had many congregations and meetings all over the city. The local church in Corinth was the church throughout the city.

Household churches

Domestic households were larger in New Testament times and were seen as communities in their own right, so churches naturally developed within these social structures. There were no formal church buildings then, so homes were the obvious place for believers to meet.

We can helpfully call these household expressions of *ekklesia* 'community churches', and we find them mentioned in Romans 16:5; 1 Corinthians 16:19; Colossians 4:15 and Philemon 1:2.

These seem to have been fully functioning churches expressing *ekklesia*, having leadership, and doing everything that churches should do. They were not independent units but interdependent parts of the local church. Quite possibly, local church leadership was drawn from household church leaders.

In the New Testament, believers were identified as part of the local church – the church in Ephesus, Corinth and so on. But some of these churches were enormous and would themselves have consisted of many different congregations or households. So today's local congregations are generally much closer to household churches than to the other biblical expressions of *ekklesia*.

It is important we understand these distinctions so that we do not try to apply the principles and examples of New Testament local churches to modern local churches. For example, although 1 Corinthians was written to the church in Corinth (to an interdependent group of household churches) its teaching is usually applied today to individual congregations – to independent community churches.

This means that a passage like 1 Corinthians 11:18 is used by leaders to deal with divisions within their congregation rather than to heal disunity between congregations. And passages like 1 Corinthians 12:1–30 are usually applied congregationally rather than corporately.

1 Corinthians
11:18 ☐
12:1–30 ☐

Of course, every passage about the universal or local church is relevant to community churches. But the difference between the applications mentioned above is bound to be considerable.

All this underlines that there is no single complete expression of the universal church on earth. Instead there are many earthly expressions of the church. These dare not be exclusive, separate or independent – for they are joined to Christ and, through him, are joined to each other.

PRINCIPLES OF *EKKLESIA*

No New Testament church was merely an informal collection of Christians. Although relationship is at the heart of *ekklesia*, a New Testament church was about much more than informal fellowship in a large meeting or small home.

There seem to be four basic biblical principles which should operate before a group of believers can be considered a church.

1. Although equality of status and value are fundamental to the idea of *ekklesia*, this does not mean that there should also be equality of function. Greek city assemblies appointed different people to be magistrates and generals, without pretending that one was more important than the other. They had different functions but equal status and worth. It is meant to be the same in the church.

    Leadership is vital for *ekklesia*. Every body must have form and function, and leadership must be present in church life. Christ is 'the leader', and he delegates to human under-leaders the responsibility for the spiritual care and well-being of *his* members. This, however, does not mean that the leaders have a higher status and greater worth than the other members. They merely have a distinctive function. We examine this in Part Eight.

2. To be a genuine expression of *ekklesia*, a group must accept the complete charge that Christ has given to the church. Groups which meet for one or two purposes – like evangelism, healing or fellowship – are not a proper church. Church means doing *everything* we study in Part Nine.

3. There cannot be an identifiable church without identified members. Greek city assemblies had complete lists of the free men of the city, and they all had particular rights, responsibilities and duties. It is absolutely basic to the idea of *ekklesia* that everyone knows who is and who is not a member of the gathering. Leaders are called to train members for ministry; this is impossible without some form of visible and active membership.

    New Testament believers, however, were members of a household church *and* a local church *and* the universal church; and we need to work hard at developing and encouraging a similar tripartite approach to church membership.

4. No expression of the church is an isolated group cut off from the rest of the body. There is only 'One Church', and each expression of *ekklesia* should be in partnership with all the other parts. Unity and co-operation are vital for any credible expression of *ekklesia*.

THE CHALLENGE OF *EKKLESIA*

These four principles, and the Greek and Old Testament backgrounds to *ekklesia*, challenge many different attitudes and practices which are common in today's churches. In particular, we need to work carefully through the following three basic issues if we are to have a truly biblical understanding of the church.

Buildings

Even though most modern believers know that 'the church' is not the building, many still behave as if the building is the heart of the church. Too often, what occurs in the building is all there is to their church.

Building-bound thinking restricts the church, for a building's size, shape and structure can limit and hinder activities. Any church whose vision is governed by its building is hardly a biblical church.

Obviously, we need buildings in our European climate and culture, but they are tools which should neither be reverenced nor allowed to replace the church's real identity.

We must never forget that the early church did not have any purpose-built buildings – and most of the fast-growing churches in Africa, Latin America and Asia do not have impressive or extravagant buildings.

Meetings

Some modern believers confuse 'church' with 'meetings' in the same way that many translations of the Bible confuse *qahal* with *edah*. It is almost as if they think that they fulfil the church's purpose by having ever more meetings.

But if 'church' is limited to meetings, the church ceases to be when the meeting ends. This is exactly how many believers behave. When they leave the meeting (or the building), they feel that they have left the church until their next visit or meeting.

We are not *ekklesia*, however, because we gather together; we gather together because we are *ekklesia*. Church is both an eternal relationship and a series of earthly responsibilities, and most churches seem to lose power and vitality when their life and mission are formalised mainly in meetings.

Organisations

The church is a living organism which owes its life to God and not to human organisation. It is the church of God, and it exists only by his grace, power and sovereign initiative. Like buildings and meetings, organisation must have a role in working out *ekklesia*, but it should not dominate.

Excessive organisation leads to unhelpful methods, a confusion of goals and cumbersome structures. Institutional goals can replace spiritual aims. Commercial motives and secular practices creep in. Ambition replaces service. Hierarchical leadership structures are borrowed from business life. And over-organisation slowly squeezes life and flexibility from the church.

Throughout history, God has gone on breathing fresh life into his church by his Spirit. Believers have always liked spiritual renewal; but then they have organised it; and finally they have regimented it. God's plan for the church is continuous renewal on an unceasing journey to a glorious destiny. We are always meant to be moving on with God, but this is frequently frustrated by our human love of organisation, conservation and preservation.

From the smallest household church to the largest city church, every expression of *ekklesia* must be led by Christ. *Ekklesia* – the highest example of God's will and purpose on earth, the body within which he has chosen to reveal his glory to all the nations – should be served and facilitated by organisation, not dominated, manipulated or stifled by it.

By definition, a gathered and gathering church should always be on the move. It should always be seeking for relevant ways of releasing captives, revealing glory, and relating in love to one other. We should always be pressing on to the promised inheritance of glory which God holds out before us.

PART FOUR

the fellowship

While *ekklesia* is the main Greek word which the New Testament uses to identify 'the church', there is a second important group of Greek words which the Bible also uses to describe the church.

Koinos is the Greek word which means 'common', and a family of words based in this root-word are used in relation to the church.

- *Koinonia* means 'sharing together with a clear common purpose', and is translated in various places as 'fellowship', 'communion', 'communication', 'contribution' and 'distribution'. We see this, for example, in Philemon 1:6; 2 Corinthians 6:14; Romans 15:26; 2 Corinthians 9:13 & Acts 2:42.

- *Koinonos* means 'a person who shares together with others in a common purpose' and is translated in the New Testament as 'companion', 'partner' and 'partaker'. It appears in Hebrews 10:33; 1 Peter 5:1 & Luke 5:10.

- *Koinoneo* means 'to share together' and is translated as either 'to have fellowship' or 'to communicate'. Although fellowship is not a verb in English, 'to fellowship' is the literal way of rendering this.

Philemon 1:6 ☐

2 Corinthians 6:14 ☐

Romans 15:26 ☐

2 Corinthians 9:13

Acts 2:42 ☐

Hebrews 10:33 ☐

1 Peter 5:1 ☐

Luke 5:10 ☐

- *Sunkoinonos* means 'a person who shares together with others in a clearly identified common purpose'. It is translated as 'a companion in' and 'a partaker in'. It appears in Romans 11:17; 1 Corinthians 9:23; Philippians 1:7 & Revelation 1:9.

- *Sunkoinoneo* means 'to share together with or in something' and is translated as 'to have fellowship with', 'to share in', 'to partake of' and 'to communicate with'. We see this in Ephesians 5:11; Philippians 4:14 & Revelation 18:4.

The *koionos* word group shows that, as believers, we share together in the things of God. This is 'the fellowship, or communion, of saints', and is the reason why 'fellowship' so accurately describes the church.

Like *ekklesia*, *koinonia* refers to the relationship we have – by the cross and by the Spirit – with God and with each other. Some modern believers consider *koinonia* to be one of the church's activities: what happens at the end of the services. But fellowship encircles everything that we have, are and do as believers. It is another word for church – which is why some groups refer to themselves as 'The Fellowship'.

WHAT IS FELLOWSHIP?

Just as many people's ideas about 'church' often bear little resemblance to *ekklesia*, so it is with 'fellowship' and *koinonia*. Whatever springs into our minds when someone mentions fellowship may well be far removed from the New Testament meaning of *koinonia*.

The simplest way of understanding biblical fellowship is 'sharing with someone in something'. This means that there are two basic requirements for scriptural fellowship:

1. A sense of 'gathering together' is essential, for it is impossible to have fellowship on our own, in isolation. As with everything to do with the church, fellowship is corporate: it is based on relationships.

2. There must be a common purpose at the root, for it is impossible to have purposeless fellowship. Fellowship means 'participation in something with others', rather than just 'association with others'.

These two basic requirements should revolutionise our understanding of fellowship – and, perhaps, cause us to rename those after-service cups of coffee!

In the New Testament, 'fellowship' is described in three complementary ways.

- *having a share in something*

- *giving a share in something*

- *sharing in something with someone*

We need to appreciate that biblical fellowship involves all these aspects of sharing, and not just one or two of them.

Having a share

In the New Testament, this refers to the following:

- *partners in a common enterprise or business* – 2 Corinthians 8:4, 23; Luke 5:10

- *sharing in a common experience* – for example, persecution, Hebrews 10:33; Revelation 1:9; suffering, 2 Corinthians 1:7; worship, 1 Corinthians 10:18; murder, Matthew 23:30

- *sharing in a common privilege* – Romans 11:17; 1 Corinthians 9:23

- *sharing in a common spiritual reality* – Philippians 1:7; 1 Peter 5:1; 2 Peter 1:4

- *sharing in sin* – Ephesians 5:11; 1 Timothy 5:22; 2 John 1:11; Revelation 18:4

- *sharing in a common spiritual activity* – 1 Corinthians 10:16

- *sharing in and with God himself* – 1 Corinthians 1:9; 2 Corinthians 13:14; Philippians 2:1; 3:10; 1 John 1:3

Giving a share

Although New Testament fellowship usually refers to 'having a share in something with someone', there are several passages where it means 'giving a share in something to someone'. This suggests that fellowship is closely related to generosity and grace.

2 Corinthians 8:4 ☐
8:23 ☐

Luke 5:10 ☐

Hebrews 10:33 ☐

Revelation 1:9 ☐

2 Corinthians 1:7 ☐

1 Corinthians 10:18 ☐

Matthew 23:30 ☐

Romans 11:17 ☐

1 Corinthians 9:23 ☐

Philippians 1:7 ☐

1 Peter 5:1 ☐

2 Peter 1:4 ☐

Ephesians 5:11 ☐

1 Timothy 5:22 ☐

2 John 1:11 ☐

Revelation 18:4 ☐

1 Corinthians 10:16 ☐

1 Corinthians 1:9 ☐

2 Corinthians 13:14 ☐

Philippians 2:1 ☐
3:10 ☐

Romans 15:26 ☐

2 Corinthians 8:4 ☐

9:13 ☐

Philippians 1:5 ☐

Philemon 1:6 ☐

Acts 2:44 ☐

4:32 ☐

Galatians 2:9 ☐

1 Corinthians 1:9 ☐

We see this link in Romans 15:26; 2 Corinthians 8:4 & 9:13. And it is probably the meaning behind Philippians 1:5 and Philemon 1:6.

These last two passages make most sense when we interpret them as Paul thanking God for Philemon's and the Philippians' generous financial support of the ministry of the gospel, rather than thanking God that they were actually preaching the gospel.

The context around Acts 2:44 and 4:32 also suggests that the fellowship had more to do with 'giving' than 'having'. Many leaders in the past believed that Acts 2:42 was the early church's 'order of service', and that their 'fellowship' was our 'offering'.

In Greek, however, these passages refer to 'the fellowship', which probably suggests a formally-constituted fellowship. This would have included giving, perhaps even as a principal expression of fellowship.

Sharing

One passage about 'fellowship' is less straightforward. Galatians 2:9 refers to 'the right hand of fellowship', and we do know what this precisely meant. It may have been a symbol of good will and blessing, or a symbolic gesture of unity and partnership, or even a financial gift.

Some people think that Paul's frequent use of 'fellowship' as a word for 'generous giving which supports the gospel' means that 'the right hand' was a gift from the Jerusalem leaders to fund Paul's ministry to the Gentiles, and was the reason why Paul was so keen for his Gentile converts to send a substantial gift back to the Jerusalem church.

All we can say for certain is that the use of *koinonia* in Galatians 2:9 must refer to a real sharing by the Jerusalem leaders in Paul's ministry to the Gentiles, and by Paul in their ministry to the Jews.

THE BASIS OF FELLOWSHIP

Fellowship is not something that believers do or create by their actions and attitudes. Fellowship is something that we receive from God. 1 Corinthians 1:9 reveals the divine initiative in fellowship by stating that we have been called by God into the fellowship of his Son. And 1 John 1:3–7 makes it plain that all genuine fellowship is founded in Christ. Everything that we share together as Christians we share in and through Jesus. He is the one whom we are and have in common.

1 John 1:3–7 ☐

Romans 11:17 uses poetic language to show that all Gentile believers are 'partakers', 'partners', 'fellowshippers', of the holy root – that is the Son of God. We have been grafted into the 'olive tree' of 'true Israel', whose 'root' is Christ. We cannot graft ourselves in; and our sharing in and with 'true Israel' means that the life of 'the tree' and 'the root' – of 'true Israel' and 'the Son' – begins to flow through us. We consider this aspect of fellowship more fully in Part Six.

Romans 11:17 ☐

Philippians 1:2 indicates that true fellowship is also accomplished by the Spirit – who is himself the Spirit of fellowship. Through the Spirit, we participate in the Son; and, through the Spirit, we are in relationship with all believers – Jewish and Gentile – who live in him.

Philippians 1:2 ☐

Through the Word

In 1 John 1:2–3, fellowship begins with the revelation of God through his Son, the Word of life. The apostles passed on the good news that Jesus came to reveal the Father and to enable us to have fellowship with the Father. We shared in their revelation of the good news when we received their message – and so *koinonia* came into being.

1 John 1:2–3 ☐

1 John 5:20 indicates that this fellowship is not based on intellectual agreement, but in a knowledge – an experience – of truth. Our fellowship with the living Word, with Jesus, is drawn from the written Word, the Bible. This is also the food of our fellowship with each other in the church as we encourage and challenge one other by its teaching.

1 John 5:20 ☐

Through the cross

We know that our sins separated us from God and that Jesus died to make fellowship with God possible. Ephesians 2:13–18; 1 John 1:7 & 4:10 show that the cross establishes the basis for fellowship between God and humanity, and between people in the church.

Ephesians 2:13–18 ☐

1 John 1:7 ☐
4:10 ☐

These verses show that it is impossible to separate 'fellowship with God' from 'fellowship with each other'. The cross accomplished for humanity both a new vertical and a new horizontal relationship.

Through the Spirit

2 Corinthians
13:14 □

The well-known words of 'the grace', in 2 Corinthians 13:14, remind us that the Holy Spirit also produces and sustains our fellowship. He is the Spirit of fellowship and he brings us an understanding of the truth and a deep assurance of our relationship with God.

Because – individually – we are in him and he is in us, the Spirit shares the presence, power and purity of God with us. But because all believers are in him *together*, he unites us as God's people and enables us to share together in him and in our blessings in Christ.

THE EXPRESSION OF FELLOWSHIP

Acts 2:42 □

Acts 2:42 describes how the first converts devoted themselves to the fellowship, to *koinonia*. This does not mean the informal aspects of church life – the bits before and after meetings. *Koinonia* is, by definition, purposeful and includes *everything* that we are called to do together as Christians.

True fellowship can only be expressed within a body which is clear about its identity, purpose and function. Believers who are not fully part of a local expression of the church are seriously remiss in their relationship with Christ. So too, any congregations which are not in fellowship with other local expressions of the body are equally negligent in their relationship with the head of the church.

Fellowship can be expressed in obvious ways like prayer, worship, social activities and practical work; but the New Testament highlights five main ways that the church should express the fellowship God has given to us in Christ.

The Lord's Supper

The Lord's Supper is such a vital expression of our fellowship that it has come to be known in many parts of the church as 'holy communion'. We now know that 'communion' is one translation of *koinonia*, so it might be helpful if we sometimes called the Lord's Supper 'the fellowship meal'.

We examine the Lord's Supper in Part Ten, but we should note now that, in 1 Corinthians 10:16–17, it is God's specially ordained way of confirming our continuing fellowship with Christ in his blood and our continuing fellowship with each other in his body.

1 Corinthians 10:16–17 ☐

It is also relevant that, in 1 Corinthians 11:17 – 14:40, Paul's practical teaching on spiritual gifts, worship, the body and love is set in the context of the Lord's Supper. In the New Testament church, the regular *koinonia* meal visibly expressed all these aspects of fellowship.

1 Corinthians 11:17–14:40 ☐

Giving to the needy

We have seen that true fellowship involves 'giving a share'. Because we share together spiritually in Christ we should also want to share together materially.

Genuine *koinonia* in Christ naturally leads to physical provision for those in need – as both an expression and evidence of the fellowship. Passages like Acts 2:40–47; Romans 15:26; 1 Timothy 6:18; Hebrews 13:1 & 1 John 3:17 demonstrate that this generosity is precisely what God demands and expects. Anything less than generosity to needy Christians is a denial of fellowship and a rejection of *koinonia*.

Acts 2:40–47 ☐
Romans 15:26 ☐
1 Timothy 6:18 ☐
Hebrews 13:1 ☐
1 John 3:17 ☐

Supporting Christian ministries

Paul often described the special partnership he enjoyed with the church at the town of Philippi in the region of Macedonia. The Philippian believers repeatedly expressed their fellowship by supporting Paul's travelling ministry with prayer and finance – we see this in 2 Corinthians 8:3–4; Philippians 1:4–5 & 4:15–19.

2 Corinthians 8:3–4 ☐
Philippians 1:4–5 ☐
4:15–19 ☐

Supporting ministries in this way is an important expression of fellowship. By our giving we become 'partners' or 'fellowshippers' in the gospel with those who preach – and 2 Corinthians 9:1–15 shows how much we are blessed by God in return!

2 Corinthians 9:1–15 ☐

Enduring suffering

We must never forget that, as Christians, we are sometimes called to suffer for Christ. Whenever we do this together, or identify with and support those who are suffering, we express our fellowship in Christ.

We see this in 2 Corinthians 1:7; Philippians 3:10; 4:14; Philemon 1:7; Hebrews 10:33 & Revelation 1:9.

Passages like 1 Peter 4:13 & 1 Corinthians 12:26 explain that our union with Christ and his body means we are affected by whatever happens to our brothers and sisters. Genuine fellowship expresses this reality either in joy with the blessed or in tears with those who suffer.

Spreading the gospel

In the light of the material we have examined, it is difficult to envisage any teaching about the church which does not stress the importance of revealing glory and spreading the gospel to all nations.

In 1 Peter 5:1, the writer describes himself as 'a partaker' – a companion or fellowshipper – of the glory that will be revealed: once again, the promise of glory is held before us. And 2 Peter 1:4 claims that we are already sharers in the divine nature – which is glory.

Nearly all Paul's teaching about fellowship is set in the context of sharing the gospel – even if his explicit teaching about 'fellowship in the gospel' probably means financial support rather than preaching. Even so, 1 Corinthians 9:23; Galatians 2:9; Philippians 1:5, 7 & Philemon 1:6 show that fellowship was expressed so that the gospel could be spread more effectively.

The common purpose of our sharing is not to receive a personal blessing, it is to share dynamically the good news with the nations so that the glory of God is seen by the whole world.

PART FIVE

pictures of the church

As well as the two Greek words *ekklesia* and *koinonia*, the New Testament also uses eleven 'word pictures' to describe the church.

No one image or metaphor fully represents the church, but they offer a helpful and instructive overview of the church when they are taken together. They are:

- *the chosen people of God* – 1 Peter 2:9

- *the body of Christ* – Ephesians 1:23

- *the building of God* – 1 Corinthians 3:16

- *the bride of Christ* – 2 Corinthians 11:2

- *the family of God* – Ephesians 3:15

- *the flock of Christ* – 1 Peter 5:2

- *the city of God* – Revelation 21:2

- *the vine of Christ* – John 15:1–5

- *the army of God* – Matthew 16:18–19

1 Peter 2:9 ☐

- *the royal priesthood* – 1 Peter 2:9

- *the holy nation* – 1 Peter 2:9

It should be clear that a sense of 'gathering' and of 'common purpose' – of *ekklesia* and *koinonia* – are basic to each of these pictures. But a further three emphases are also implied within each of the images. They are:

1.   the corporate nature of the church

2.   the relationship between God and his people

3.   the function that God has given to his church

As we examine each picture in turn, we should watch out for these emphases and consider what they mean for our situation.

THE PEOPLE OF GOD

1 Peter 2:9 describes the church as *'a chosen people'*. We are those men and women who have been carefully chosen from all other people to belong to God. He really has chosen us, called us and gathered us together and to himself. His word cannot be broken. His love never fails. And we have been summoned to an exclusive and intimate relationship with him.

But this was not a new revelation in the New Testament. The constant message throughout the Bible is that God has always desired a people – a community – that will share his life. We have already seen this in Exodus 6:7, and it runs on throughout the Old and New Testaments to Revelation 21:3.

Exodus 6:7 ☐

Revelation 21:3 ☐

God's people of Israel

In the Old Testament, the people of Israel were 'the people of God'. They had been chosen by him and brought into a covenant relationship with him. Their lives were bound up in God's.

Israel did not choose to become God's people, God chose them. *He* redeemed them from slavery; *he* gave them the Law and the covenant;

he led them into Canaan and gave them a kingdom; *he* sent them his prophets, rescued them from exile, and gave them his Son. It was all God's sovereign grace at work, as he showered love on his people.

In contrast, the people of Israel responded to God's grace with disobedience, sin, failure, rebellion, complaints, betrayal, rejection and apostasy. In his love, God punished them, but this was always shot through with mercy and a promise of restoration. We see this, for example, in Hosea 11:7–11.

Hosea 11:7–11 ☐

As we look at God's dealings with his people in the Old Testament, we see that the theme of salvation runs through everything. We see this in Ezekiel 11:19–25; 14:11; 26:25–28; Jeremiah 7:23; 24:7; 30:22 & 32:37–40.

Ezekiel 11:19–25 ☐
14:11 ☐
26:25–28 ☐

Jeremiah 7:23 ☐
24:7 ☐
30:22 ☐
32:37–40 ☐

The concept of 'God's people' is the main theme of Hosea. Through the adultery of his wife, Hosea must have felt something of God's pain at the unfaithfulness of Israel. In the first two chapters, the God-given prophetic names of Hosea's children point to Israel's rejection and salvation, and illustrate the merciful way God deals with his people. Hosea 2:21–23, however, looks forward to a day when those who then were not God's people would become his people. It points to the church, and this is taken up in 1 Peter 2:10.

Hosea 1:1–2:23 ☐

1 Peter 2:10 ☐

The church, by faith in the Messiah, was adopted into the 'true Israel' – which became the real people of God drawn from every nation whom he had always desired. When we read Acts, we see how the Spirit led the first Jewish believers into the truth that the gospel was not limited to them. Time and again this is a theme in Paul's letters, for example, Romans 9:6–8; Galatians 3:6–8; 6:16.

Romans 9:6–8 ☐

Galatians 3:6–8 ☐
6:16 ☐

The rejection of the nation of Israel, and the adoption of the church into the faithful remnant within Israel, underline God's sovereignty and salvation. It is all God's initiative and all Christ's work. We see this in Luke 1:16–17, 68–77; 2:10 & 31–32, and examine it in the next chapter.

Luke 1:16–17 ☐
1:68–77 ☐
2:10 ☐
2:31–32 ☐

Being God's people

Deuteronomy 4:5–6 makes it plain that Israel was not called to be God's people merely so that they could enjoy God's favour. They had to keep God's law in the land they were entering 'in the sight of the peoples'. Through Israel's obedience, God would be glorified in the eyes of other nations.

Deuteronomy
4:5–6 ☐

Like Israel, the church has been called to be God's community or society in the world. We are called to obey and serve him 'in the land, in the sight of the peoples'.

1 Peter 2:9–4:19 □

All the practical teaching in 1 Peter 2:11–4:19 flows from being God's people in 1 Peter 2:9. This shows that our personal and corporate behaviour is meant 'to proclaim the praises of him who called us': it is meant to result in glory.

Quite simply, it has always been God's will and purpose that his people should glorify him in the world. We have been called to reveal him in the church – through our life as his people – to the world that does not know him. We see this in Matthew 5:14–16; 2 Corinthians 6:16–18 & Titus 2:11–14.

Matthew 5:14–16 □

2 Corinthians
6:16–18 □

Titus 2:11–14 □

Being the people of God today means working out our corporate life in a world which emphasises the personal and individual. This is not easy, but we must always remember and emphasise that we are 'the people of God' not 'the individuals of God'.

Every picture of the church stresses the essential corporate nature of the church, yet modern believers still talk about *my* faith, *my* belief, *my* salvation, *my* church, *my* relationship with God, and so on.

And many leaders apply the New Testament teaching about, for example, the work and gifts of the Spirit, spiritual warfare and guidance in an individualistic way, and teach from the epistles as though they were written for individual believers. This is not so.

Somehow the church has to rediscover what it means to be 'the people of God'. It is time to grasp that *we* are citizens of his heaven; *we* are children of his kingdom; *we* are subject to his laws and *we* are directed by his Spirit. Together, *we* are the Lord's.

THE BODY OF CHRIST

Ephesians 1:23 □

Ephesians 1:23 describes the church as *'his body'*. Although many believers are unfamiliar with the idea of the church as God's people, most are used to thinking about the church Christ's body, Not all, however, work through this idea and live under the headship of Christ.

The body picture is not mentioned in the Old Testament, the Gospels or Acts, but is used by Paul in many of his letters. At that time, the Greek word *soma*, 'body', was commonly used to describe the unity of anything which consisted of many members – a Senate, for example -and so was an obvious word to use of the church.

In the New Testament, 'the body of Christ' is used in three ways:

- *the death of Christ on the cross* – Romans 7:4; Hebrews 10:10

- *the fellowship experienced in the Lord's Supper* – 1 Corinthians 10:16; 11:23–29

- *the body of believers*, whose oneness was made possible through the cross and is expressed in the *koinonia* meal – Romans 12:4–5; Ephesians 1:23; Colossians 1:18–24

Oneness

Paul never refers to the body of Christians or the body of believers, but always to the body of Christ. This must mean that he is referring to a form of the organic oneness he mentions in Ephesians 2:15–16, and that he is demanding the church be ruled by Christ as head.

The body picture goes further than the people picture – which shows we belong to God and one another. The body picture, however, teaches that we also abide in Christ, find our life in him, and are directed by him. Without Christ, there is no life, no hope, no church.

This picture stresses that Jesus is our head and we are his body. We are vitally connected to him and mutually dependent with all other believers on him. We do Christ's work under his direction, and each member has a unique and indispensable part to play.

Of course, as God, Christ exists apart from the church, but 1 Corinthians 12:12 shows just how closely linked the church is with the Son. He might exist apart from us but we cannot exist apart from him.

Universal and local

In Ephesians 1:23; 2:16; 4:4, 12, 16, 5:23, 30; Colossians 1:18; 2:17–23 and 3:15, 'the body' clearly refers to the universal church – which we considered earlier.

Romans 7:4 ☐

Hebrews 10:10 ☐

1 Corinthians
10:16 ☐
11:23–29 ☐

Romans 12:4–5 ☐

Ephesians 1:23 ☐

Colossians
1:18–24 ☐

Ephesians
2:15–16 ☐

1 Corinthians
12:12 ☐

Ephesians 1:23 ☐
2:16 ☐
4:4 ☐
4:12–16 ☐
5:23, 30 ☐

Colossians 1:18 ☐
2:17–23 ☐
3:15 ☐

Romans 12:4–5 ☐

1 Corinthians
        10:16–17 ☐
        12:12–27 ☐

In Romans 12:4–5; 1 Corinthians 10:16–17 and 12:12–27, however, Paul seems to be identifying the local church – the city-wide community of household churches – as the body of Christ.

Although many congregations refer to themselves as 'the body', a household or community church is never described as the body of Christ in the New Testament. A local 'body', however, is a 'local' or 'community' *expression* of the one body of Christ.

In writing to the church in Corinth, Paul was seeking to correct divisions *between* congregations in the city over leaders, gifts, ministries and the Lord's Supper. His teaching about the body reminds them that, *together*, they are the body of Christ in Corinth, and that the different congregational groups need each other.

We have seen that each expression of the church is not 'the church', but it is a full representation of the body in that place. As Colossians 2:10 shows, every expression of the church is 'complete in him'.

Colossians 2:10 ☐

We know that the whole gospel, the fullness of God, the finished work of Christ, every promise in the Bible, the complete gift, gifts and work of the Holy Spirit, are all fully available in every expression of 'the church'. Yet, the body teaching means that no expression is independent, they are all interdependent.

Somehow, every individual congregation needs to hold these parallel and complementary truths about the church in some sort of tension:

- *we are complete in him*

- *we urgently need all the other congregations in our locality*

Being the body

Unity, growth, work and reproduction are implicit features of the body picture. And 1 Corinthians 12 and Ephesians 4 reveal a string of implications of being the body of Christ which relate to this.

1 Corinthians 12 ☐

Ephesians 4 ☐

Being the body means being united in Christ, growing together to be like Christ, working together with Christ, and reproducing or multiplying his image. Whatever the differences between different congregations and traditions, we need each other, we belong to one another, and we must develop a strong, forgiving love for each other – 1 Corinthians 12:12–20; Ephesians 4:3.

In particular, the biblical 'body' teaching shows that we must all:

- *be involved in the work of ministry* – Ephesians 4:12

- *grow in our knowledge of Christ* – Ephesians 4:13–14

- *speak the truth in love to each other* – Ephesians 4:15, 25

- *be totally committed to each other* – Ephesians 4:15–16

- *value spiritual gifts, as they glorify God and edify the body* – 1 Corinthians 12:3–7

- *appreciate that every gift is important* – 1 Corinthians 12:21–26

- *use the gifts* – Romans 12:6

- *recognise the variety of gifts* – 1 Corinthians 12:8–10

- *eagerly and earnestly desire the gifts, especially prophecy* – 1 Corinthians 12:31

- *test the gifts* – 1 Thessalonians 5:21

- *ensure that Christ is the absolute head of every expression of the church* – Colossians 1:17–22; 2:18–19

Romans 12:6 ☐

1 Thessalonians 5:21 ☐

Colossians 1:17–22 ☐ 2:18–19 ☐

THE BUILDING OF GOD

The New Testament also uses the picture of a building to describe the church. The Old Testament tabernacle and temples are clearly behind this metaphor. The church is the place where God is, where God's people enjoy his presence and offer him prayer, praise, worship and sacrifice. As we have seen, the church is where God reveals his glory.

In particular, the church is identified as:

- *God's building* – 1 Corinthians 3:9

- *the temple of God* – 1 Corinthians 3:16; 2 Corinthians 6:16

- *Christ's house* – Hebrews 3:6; 2 Peter 2:5

- *a holy temple* – Ephesians 2:21

- *a habitation of God in the Spirit* – Ephesians 2:22

1 Corinthians 3:9 ☐ 3:16 ☐

2 Corinthians 6:16 ☐

Hebrews 3:6 ☐

2 Peter 2:5 ☐

Ephesians 2:21–22 ☐

The idea of the body and the building are related by Jesus' words in John 2:19–21. This suggests that just as the church is Christ's body, so too it must also be his temple.

Spiritual building

The tabernacle and temple were fundamental to Israel's worship, but Jesus taught – in John 4:19–24 – that a better kind of worship was coming which would be spiritual rather than physical.

Jesus explained that people would soon no longer need special, holy buildings to worship God, for they would themselves by made holy by the Holy Spirit, and they would not need to make physical sacrifices since they would themselves be living sacrifices.

Sadly, many believers still seem to think that their church building is a kind of special place, a new temple. Now, however, it is the people of God, the church, which is the temple, the building where God dwells.

In the Old Testament, God chose a tabernacle as the symbol of his presence because of its inherent mobility and flexibility. God's people moved when God moved and where God moved, and they carried the tabernacle with them.

A special building, the temple, was David's idea, and God protested about this in 2 Samuel 7:1–7. Of course, God allowed the temple to be built, much as he allowed Israel to have a king, but it was not God's original purpose that worship should focus on a fixed building.

The fact that the church is the spiritual building of God should make us think very carefully about our attitudes towards physical buildings.

Founded on Christ

The New Testament uses several pictures to show that Christ is involved in every part of the building.

He is:

- *the designer and builder* – Matthew 16:18

- *the foundation* – 1 Corinthians 3:11; Colossians 2:6–7

- *the cornerstone* – 1 Peter 2:4–8; Ephesians 2:20–22

John 2:19–21 ☐

John 4:19–24 ☐

2 Samuel 7:1–7 ☐

Matthew 16:18 ☐

1 Corinthians 3:11 ☐

Colossians 2:6–7 ☐

1 Peter 2:4–8 ☐

Ephesians 2:20–22 ☐

These verses show that a church ceases to be God's 'building' as soon as it moves away from Christ – some sort of spiritual dry rot sets in and the building begins to decay.

Created by the Spirit

Ephesians 2:22 reveals that the building is in, and through, and by, the Spirit. Without the work of the Spirit, the church cannot become the habitation of God, the place where God is.

Ephesians 2:22 ☐

Everything to do with the church depends on the Holy Spirit. It is his presence, power and purity which brings life and vitality to the church. Our worship, our praying, our preaching, our serving, our understanding – all must be 'in the Spirit'.

Constructed from living stones

1 Corinthians 3:9–17 makes it plain that we must be careful what we put into the building, as it will be tested in God's fire. And 2 Peter 2:4–5 shows that we are living stones which must be built together, on and in Christ, into a spiritual house.

1 Corinthians 3:9–17 ☐

2 Peter 2:4–5 ☐

Every stone is equally important. Each one needs to find its right place and be bonded to those around it. The whole building is weakened if any stone is not in position.

Still being built

It is important we grasp that this building is still under construction – which means that there are bound to be some 'scaffolding' and 'raw materials' lying around looking rather unattractive.

1 Corinthians 5:1–5 should be our attitude and experience, as we look forward with expectancy to 'the habitation from heaven' which is before us. Until then, however, we have the Spirit as a guarantee of the glory before us, and we should pray and work together with God so that the church becomes the house he wants: a dwelling-place which is filled with his presence, his character, his beauty, his authority, his nature, his love, his praise – in short, his glory.

1 Corinthians 5:1–5 ☐

THE BRIDE OF CHRIST

Most evangelical and pentecostal believers know that the church is Christ's bride, but few realise that the actual expression 'the bride of Christ' does not appear in the New Testament.

Revelation 22:17 □

2 Corinthians
    11:2 □

Ephesians
    5:22–33 □

Revelation 22:17 refers to 'the bride'; 2 Corinthians 11:2 infers that the church is to become the bride of Christ; and Ephesians 5:22–33 implies that the relationship between Christ and the church is like that between a husband and wife.

Isaiah 54:1–8 □
    62:4–5 □

This is another picture of the church which is rooted in the Old Testament, and it speaks of an exceptionally intimate union between God and his people. We see it, for example, in Isaiah 54:1–8 & 62:4–5.

Israel as bride

Jeremiah 3 □

Ezekiel 16 □

Hosea 2:14–20 □

As the bride of God, Israel was called into a devoted, committed and exclusive relationship with God. Disobedience or indifference were considered to be adultery – Jeremiah 3 & Ezekiel 16. Yet Hosea 2:14–20 reveals God to be still in love with his unfaithful partner.

Psalm 45 □

Song of Solomon
    4:9–11 □

The 'marriage' relationship between Israel and God is seen most clearly in Psalm 45 and Song of Solomon. If God feels for Israel as expressed in Song of Solomon 4:9–11, how much more must he feel for the church!

Mark 2:18–20 □

Matthew 22:1–14 □

Jesus uses the wedding analogy in Mark 2:18–20 and Matthew 22:1–14 to represent himself as 'the bridegroom' and the kingdom of heaven as his marriage feast.

The picture of the church as Christ's bride is thoroughly scriptural and suggests three important facts about the church.

- *the church is meant to be morally and doctrinally pure* – Ephesians 5:22–33 & 1 Corinthians 11:2–4

- *the church is passionately loved by Christ*

- *the church is meant to be deeply in love with Christ*

Revelation
    19:6–9 □

As believers, we have the glorious wedding day before us which is described in Revelation 19:6–9. This promise should fill us with hope and encourage us to prepare ourselves for that day.

OTHER PICTURES

The family of God

Ephesians 3:15 suggests that the church is 'God's family'. He is our Father, Jesus is our eldest brother, and all true believers are our brothers and sisters.

Ephesians 3:15 ☐

As Father, God provides everything the church needs for its life and work. As brothers and sisters, we are called to love and serve each other and display the family likeness to society.

The flock of Christ

1 Peter 5:2 describes the church as 'a flock'. We are God's sheep and Jesus is our 'good Shepherd'. He loves, knows, guards and cares for us. We need to stay close to him and close to each other. It is isolated sheep who are most vulnerable to wolves and thieves.

1 Peter 5:2 ☐

The city of God

Throughout Revelation, the church is called 'the city of God' – a place of government, safety, comfort, beauty and harmony. Without God, the city will not be established – and this will not fully happen until the new heavenly city comes down from above. For now, we are called to live as God's city on earth, influencing society for God until the ultimate city arrives.

Revelation 3:12 ☐
21:2 ☐
2:14 ☐
2:19 ☐

The vine of Christ

In John 15:1–5, Jesus describes himself as 'the true vine' and his apostles as the branches. This picture helps us to appreciate our essential unity with Christ and each other. It also shows that fruitfulness comes from remaining an intimate part of the one true vine.

John 15:1–5 ☐

The army of God

There are several New Testament passages like Matthew 16:18–19; Ephesians 6:10–20 & 1 Peter 5:8 which show that the church has a clear military function. Although the church is never specifically named

Matthew
16:18–19 ☐
Ephesians
6:10–20 ☐
1 Peter 5:8 ☐

in the New Testament as 'an army', it is clear that Jesus expects his people to be involved together in some form of spiritual warfare. This picture is based in all the Old Testament passages which describe Israel fighting against its enemies.

A royal priesthood

1 Peter 2:9 □

1 Peter 2:9 identifies the church as 'a royal priesthood'. This shows that we have been called together to serve the king by sacrificially serving the king's people in all sorts of ways, but especially through prayer and praise.

A holy nation

1 Peter 2:9 also calls the church 'a holy nation'. This suggests that we have been set aside for a corporate life of dedication and consecration.

More importantly, it reveals that our common identity in Christ supersedes our natural heritage, culture and racial origin. Our primary allegiance is to God's nation rather than to our natural nation.

The church

The church is not fully represented by any one of these pictures, and none of them should be over-emphasised. But, taken together and held in balance, they provide an extremely helpful overview of the church.

The Old Testament background to the pictures helps us to see the church's place in God's eternal plan. It is most important to note, however, the way that all the metaphors stress the corporate nature of the church, emphasise the relationship between God and his people, and point to the different functions God has given to his church.

PART SIX

the church and the kingdom

We have looked at the glorious destiny of the church, and have established some basic over-arching scriptural principles about the church. We have also considered the biblical words and pictures for the church and have noted the principles that they teach.

Before we move on to study the scriptural teaching about the church's structure, leadership, life and activities, we need to make sure that we do not confuse the church with some other biblical ideas.

WHAT IS THE KINGDOM?

The Rule of God in this *Sword of the Spirit* series sets out the biblical teaching about the kingdom in some detail.

The Greek word for kingdom, *basileia*, means 'sovereignty', 'royal power', 'kingly authority' – the activity of ruling. It does not mean the country or people ruled by a king: quite simply, the kingdom is *not* the church.

When we think about 'kingdom' in English today, we tend to mean a country or nation. But *basileia* means 'God's reign' rather than 'God's realm'. It describes an activity of God, rather than a nation, a place or a people. 'Kingdom thinking' turns our attention away from ourselves, away from the church, and towards the King of kings.

This use of 'kingdom' as a ruling activity is seen in passages like Psalm 22:28; 103:19; 145:8–13 & Daniel 4:25. It is especially clear in the New Testament – for example, Matthew 6:10 & Luke 11:2.

The present kingdom

We have noted that Jesus hardly mentions 'the church'; but 'the kingdom' dominates his teaching. He began his ministry by announcing in Mark 1:14–15 that the time had come and the kingdom of God was at hand. In Matthew 12:28 & Luke 11:20, Jesus repeated his claim that the kingdom had come and evidenced this by casting out demons. This showed that the kingdom of heaven had broken into the rule of the evil one, and that the true king was more powerful than the usurper.

The kingdom came in and with Jesus, and was the main theme of his ministry. As Messiah, Jesus is central to everything the Gospels announce about the kingdom, and the kingdom is central to everything Jesus teaches.

The future kingdom

As well as teaching that the kingdom had come, that it was 'now', Jesus also taught that the kingdom was 'not yet'. Many of the kingdom benefits, in Matthew 5:1–10, are set in the future. Although 'the blessed' already possess the kingdom, there is something still to come in the future – comfort, inheritance, mercy and so on.

Jesus' prayer in Matthew 6:10 is also both present and future. If the kingdom had fully come, we would not need to pray for it to come.

In Matthew 7:21–22, Jesus refers to a future day of reckoning when speaking about entering the kingdom. It is much the same in Matthew 8:11 & Luke 13:28–29. Throughout his ministry, Jesus continually looked forward to a day when the kingdom would come in its fullness. We see this in Matthew 13:42–43; 16:27–28; 20:21; 26:29; Mark 9:1; 10:37; 14:25 & Luke 22:18.

Whenever we think about the kingdom, we must keep these two elements in mind. The kingdom is both 'now' and 'not yet'. We experience God's rule now, but we also look forward to knowing it in the future. There is much for us now, but there is more still to come.

If we are to understand the kingdom – the personal rule of God – rightly, we must appreciate four basic principles.

1. *It belongs to God* – it is the kingdom *of God*. It is an ongoing sovereign activity of God. He is in charge. He alone rules.

2. *It is dynamic and powerful* – the kingdom is not a temporary experiment. It is the permanent coming of the all-powerful king to rule his people and rout his enemies.

3. *It is established by Jesus* – Luke 1:32–33 introduces Jesus as the one who will occupy David's throne and whose kingdom will never end. Throughout the Gospels, the kingdom and the Son of Man are inseparably linked – for example, Matthew 16:28 & Mark 9:1.

   Luke 1:32–33 ☐

   Matthew 16:28 ☐

   Mark 9:1 ☐

4. *It is for salvation* – the coming of the kingdom shows God's kingly activity in reaching out to save and bless people of every nation. The driving out of devils evidences the king's power; the healings demonstrate his compassion; but the forgiveness of sins is the most prominent miracle in the kingdom – for example, Luke 5:20–21.

   Luke 5:20–21 ☐

THE KINGDOM IN THE NEW TESTAMENT

'The kingdom' is by far the most dominant theme in Jesus' teaching and is frequently mentioned in the Gospels. The phrase 'the kingdom' does not appear that often in the rest of the New Testament, but the concept of the active personal rule of God in Christ runs throughout the New Testament. The idea of 'the lordship of Christ' is often used instead of the phrase 'the kingdom', but this merely expresses the same 'God ruling' truth in different words.

When we study the way that the New Testament mentions 'the kingdom', we see that a few basic themes run through the teaching: for example, present and future elements, opposition, salvation, inheritance, the Word of God, and the grace of God.

New Testament teaching about the kingdom includes the following:

- *seeing and entering the kingdom are linked with being born again* – John 3:1–21

- *physical and spiritual kingship are distinguished* – John 18:33–38

- *the kingdom is the content of preaching and testimony* – Acts 19:8; 20:25 & 28:23. (Acts normally uses 'the word of the Lord' to sum up preaching – as in 19:10 – and these two phrases mean the same thing.)

- *the kingdom is paralleled with 'the gospel of grace' and with teaching about Jesus* – Acts 20:24–25; 28:23 & 28:31

- *the kingdom is not about rules and regulations* – Romans 14:17

- *the kingdom is not a matter of talk* – 1 Corinthians 4:20

- *members are expected to live worthy of God* – 1 Thessalonians 2:12

- *the future inheritance of the kingdom is a basis for moral behaviour* – 1 Corinthians 6:9–10; Galatians 5:21 & Ephesians 5:5

- *the kingdom is not entered through human effort* – 1 Corinthians 15:50

- *the kingdom is the goal of missionary work* – Colossians 4:11

- *the kingdom is linked with salvation, forgiveness and a dynamic overthrow of evil powers* – Colossians 1:13–14

- *the kingdom is present and future* – 1 Corinthians 15:24–28 & Hebrews 12:28

- *the kingdom is opposed, but will be fully established* – Revelation 1:9; 11:15; 12:10. The glorious vision of the New Jerusalem is presented as the fulfilment of all the biblical promises about a future kingdom.

Acts 1:3 shows that Jesus taught about the kingdom between his resurrection and ascension. It was one thing for the disciples to try and understand the personal rule of God when Jesus was present in person. But how would the kingdom, the rule of God, work when Jesus was no longer with them in person?

Presumably Jesus told them how to live and what to preach, for Acts 17:7 shows they carried on proclaiming Jesus as king. The rule of God gripped the lives of the early Christians and characterised the message they proclaimed. Jesus was their ruler – whether they expressed this as a 'king' to the Jews, or 'the Lord' (the Caesar) to the Gentiles.

THE KINGDOM AND THE CHURCH

Many believers mistakenly think that 'the kingdom' and 'the church' are the same thing. Clearly there is a connection between the kingdom and the church, but the two are not the same. The kingdom is not a way of looking at or describing the church.

The church is the 'gathering' of all people who belong to Christ – those alive on earth and those already with him in heaven. Whereas the kingdom is the whole activity of God in Christ in the world.

Christ is central to both the kingdom and the church. 'The church', however, draws our attention to the results of his activity – to the bride, the body, and so on; whereas 'the kingdom' focuses us on him personally and on his activity.

The church is the 'fellowship' of those who have heard his call and have believed the gospel of the kingdom. We are those who 'participate' in the salvation of the kingdom and look forward to the inheritance of the kingdom. But we are not the kingdom.

The kingdom, however, does take its visible form in the church. We are called to demonstrate the kingdom by God's words, by good works and by signs and wonders. We are the light of the world, the salt of the earth, those who live by the king's rule and learn only from him. As such, the church is a tool or channel of influence of the kingdom: we carry out the kingdom's activities by living under the rule of the king.

Put another way, we can say that we are meant to be ruled by God, but we are not – and never can be – the rule of God. Many errors in church thinking and practice have arisen through confusing the church with the kingdom.

The kingdom has come. Christ is king. And he is as much a king where the church is weak and feeble as where it is strong and thriving. His kingship does not depend on the state of the church, for it is his by right. Instead, the church relies on the kingdom.

This means that, in the church, we are called to preach the kingdom to the world, to pray for the kingdom to come in glory, and always to be directed by the kingdom – yet we can never *become* the kingdom.

The early believers did not urge people to join the church, they pleaded with them to receive the kingdom and to be ruled by the king.

Belonging to the church is a consequence of entering the kingdom, of submitting to the rule of God; and this underlines that our focus should be on the kingdom and the king rather than on the church.

'Kingdom thinking' – focusing on the reign of God, concentrating on *his* activities – is one of the ways by which we can be liberated from a pre-occupation with 'our' congregation, 'our' denomination', 'our' tradition'. It helps to free us from the shackles of the independent local church approach so that we look beyond ourselves and our situation.

In reality, the early church emphasis on city-wide networks of interdependent community churches is only a practical possibility when church leaders and believers are far more concerned with 'his kingdom' than 'their' church.

THE CHURCH, THE KINGDOM AND ISRAEL

In Old Testament times, God used the people of Israel to reveal his glory to the world and establish his rule on earth. We know, however, that most people in Israel rejected God's ruler when he came in person. God's kingdom continued in Christ, but now it was open to all people of all nations.

Romans 9–11 ☐

Paul's great chapters about Israel, Romans 9–11, show that God has not finished with Israel just because it has rejected Christ, but they make it very plain that God's way of extending his kingdom rule on earth is now through the church rather than the nation of Israel.

Throughout this book, we have tried to root our understanding of the church in God's dealings with his people of Israel before Pentecost. Many modern believers, however, strongly disagree about the precise relationship between Israel and the church, and this affects the way that they apply Old Testament teaching to the church.

If we want to understand the Scriptures about this matter, we need to test the positions which people hold, to make sure that we use biblical imagery correctly, and to check that we have an overview of biblical teaching which does not focus too much on a few isolated verses.

The two commonest views that believers hold about this are:

1.   they fully identify Israel and the church

This group suggests that there is one over-arching covenant which flows through the story of God's dealings with his people; and that we see this in the Old Testament in Israel, and in the New Testament in the church. They argue that all God's dealings with Israel exactly foreshadow his dealings with the church.

As we have seen, Israel is a picture of the church. But we should not treat the story of the nation of Israel as nothing more than a foreshadowing of the church. We have noted that God dealt in grace and salvation with Israel, but we have also recognised that there are huge contrasts between the Mosaic law and the new age of grace in Christ. We look at this more fully in Part Five of *The Rule of God* and Part Ten of *Ministry in the Spirit*.

This approach leads believers to try to apply all the Old Testament teaching about Israel to the church today. People in this group often assume that all God's rules for Israel still apply to the church. We have seen, however, that this is completely inconsistent with New Testament teaching.

2.   they fully separate Israel from the church

This group suggests that Israel and the church are two totally different entities, and that God has two contrasting purposes for two quite separate peoples. As a result, they tend to overlook the Old Testament lessons for the church and concentrate almost entirely on the New Testament teaching about the church.

Some believers who hold this view are completely unconcerned about Israel, while many others are over-interested in the nation of Israel today. They imply that God is establishing his rule on earth today through both the church and the present-day nation of Israel, and suggest that the church should blindly support all the actions of Israel.

Israel – national and spiritual

In the Bible, the word 'Israel' always refers to Jewish people. In Romans 9:6, however, 'Israel' is used in two contrasting manners, and many people use it as the basis for the way they interpret the word 'Israel' throughout the rest of the Scriptures.

Romans 9:6 ☐

The most straightforward way of understanding Romans 9:6 is by recognising that it refers only to Jews, for it is in the middle of a passage which is about God's dealings with Jews. The idea that this verse establishes that we should interpret some biblical references to 'Israel' as 'the church' is not credible.

What Romans 9:6 does show, however, is that there is a difference between Jews – between 'believing' Jews and 'unbelieving' Jews, between 'national' Israel and 'spiritual' Israel. We can say Romans 9:6 reveals that not all Jews are believers – but we cannot say it shows that all believers are Jews.

The 'remnant', the 'graft' and the 'broken branches'

To grasp correctly the relationship between Israel and the church, we must understand three biblical ideas – the remnant, the graft, and the broken branches.

Romans 11:5 ☐

The Old Testament shows that, as the story of Israel developed, believing Jews became a 'remnant' within 'national Israel': this is referred to in Romans 11:5. At Pentecost, the blessing of God came upon this 'remnant' – on God's true believers, all of whom were from Israel.

Jeremiah 31 ☐

It is important we grasp that God's new covenant in Christ was made with the believing remnant in the nation of Israel. This had long been prophesied: Jeremiah 31 describes God's covenant with Israel, the breaking of the covenant by Israel, and God's promise, in 31–34, to make a new covenant with 'the house of Israel'.

Romans 11:17–24 ☐

Romans 11:17–24 explains that Gentile believers were then grafted onto the same holy root as Jews so that we could partake of the root and the fatness of the tree. This does mean that we have become part of God's believing people and that we benefit from all God's promises to the Jews; but it does not mean that we have become Jews or part of the nation of Israel.

Over the centuries, the number of believing Jews declined until they were only a tiny remnant at Pentecost. But then they were wonderfully enlarged by the 'grafting in' of faith-filled Gentile believers. This suggests that is helpful to think of the church as 'believing Jews plus a Gentile graft'. It also means that we must completely reject the false idea that the church has somehow 'replaced' Israel in God's purposes.

God's believing people were originally all Jewish, and millions of Gentiles have been grafted onto their Jewish root to benefit from their promises and spiritual heritage. We must recognise, however, that we have not been grafted onto the branches of 'national Israel' which have broken off from God's tree.

The faithful, remnant of believing Jews have, by the cross, been reconciled and made one with faith-filled Gentile believers, so that a 'new nation', a 'new habitation of God in the Spirit', now exists.

Galatians 3:28 ☐

Ephesians 2:11–22 ☐

We know, however, that the nation of Israel still exists. We must accept the teaching of Romans 11 that Israel has rejected Christ and is now a branch which has broken off from God's tree.

Romans 11:25–27 ☐

But Israel's rejection of Christ is neither total nor final. Romans 11:25–27 promises that Jews will turn to Jesus, and that – by faith in Christ – they will be grafted back again into God's holy tree.

This promise does not mean that we should support unthinkingly all the actions of Israel. Instead, we should intercede with God to keep his promise, and should wage spiritual war so that the obstacles blocking the promise's fulfilment are removed.

A right understanding of these three pictures helps us to appreciate that the church cannot be either fully identified with, or fully separated from, Israel. The truth is that we are separated from the broken branches *and* identified with the holy root. This illustrates how careful we must be in our speaking and thinking about the church and Israel.

One people

In *Ministry in the Spirit*, we see that all the blessing of God to Abraham, and all the blessings to Israel for its obedience, apply to all true believing Christians: we also see that none of the Jewish curses for disobedience apply to us. Truly the gospel is 'good news'!

There has always been only one believing people of God. At one stage in history, God's people were all drawn from the nation of Israel; but then the day of Matthew 21:43 dawned, and the people of God ceased to be totally identified with that nation.

Matthew 21:43 ☐

The Jewish leaders and law lost their authority when the era of the kingdom of God, of the personal rule of God, began. Jesus started to build his church – his new nation, the new people of God – on the root of believing Jews. And, at the cross, one new man was built from the 'remnant' and what would be 'the graft'. Finally, one day, unbelieving, faithless, Jews will turn to Christ and will be grafted back into God's true people – and then Jesus will return!

We must understand that there has only ever been one people of God; before Pentecost we call it 'Israel', and since Pentecost we call it 'the church'.

The church may be a 'new nation', but we must never forget the Jewish root onto which we have been grafted. As we saw in Part One, we simply cannot understand the church properly if we ignore the Old Testament and focus entirely on the New Testament.

The church is central to the purposes of God in these days, but we are only one stage in the story which began with Abraham, and which will continue until we reach our glorious destiny. To appreciate fully God's purpose for the church, we do need some understanding of the broad-sweep of God's dealings with his people across the generations.

THE CHURCH AND THE STATE

Many English believers belong to 'the Church of England', and most of them struggle to work out the implications of belonging to a 'state church'; large numbers of North American believers pray and work for their national and state laws to fall into line with their under-standing of biblical morality; and vast numbers of believers in Africa and Asia have to coexist with governments which are basically hostile to the church.

In fact, we can say that there is hardly an expression of the contemporary world-wide church which does not have to work hard at the vexed question of how it should relate to the state.

As with 'the church and Israel' many believers either *identify* 'the church' with 'the state' or *oppose* 'the church' to 'the state'. Before we can think about the structure and activities of the church, we need to make sure that we relate the church and the state in a biblical manner. This side of heaven, none of us can exist in the church without also existing in a state.

Whether we realise it or not, the way we structure the church and arrange our activities largely depends on the way we think about the relationship between the church and the state.

The Old Testament background

The nations surrounding Israel each had their own gods and their own religion: we can say that 'state' and 'religion' were totally identified with each other. The state ruler was also the religious ruler, and he had to be obeyed in matters of faith: we see this, for example, in Daniel 3. Everyone who was part of the nation had to belong to the religion, and anyone who did not follow the religion was persecuted.

Daniel 3:1–23 ☐

It was not much different in Israel. When Ahab made Baal-worship the new state religion, he persecuted God's prophets. In response, Elijah announced God's judgement and killed the prophets of Baal. There was room for only one religion – anything else had to go.

All Israel's wars had a religious purpose, the Jewish ruler was a religious figure, and people had to emigrate if they wanted to change religion: citizenship of the state and involvement in the religion were therefore inseparable.

Jesus' revolution

Jesus' response to a trick question about taxation, in Matthew 22:15–22, introduced a revolutionary change in attitude to the 'one state, one religion' approach of the Old Testament.

Matthew 22:15–22 ☐

If he said 'Yes', he would have been sanctioning Caesar's authority and, by implication, Caesar's religion. If he said, 'No', he would have been obeying the Mosaic law of Deuteronomy 17:14–15, but in dreadful trouble with the Romans.

Deuteronomy 17:14–15 ☐

As ever, Jesus showed that his personal authority was greater than the Law, and – for the first time in the history of the world – he separated *the claims* of state and religion.

Instead of speaking about 'one state, one religion', Jesus instructed people to abide by the distinctive authorities of Caesar and God in their parallel realms. He was not asking us to carve our lives into two sections – a 'spiritual life' and a 'secular life'. Rather, he was ordering us to live one godly life, and to learn to distinguish – and obey – different, overlapping, areas of authority over our 'one' life.

Jesus' words mean that 'church' and 'state' should be quite distinct in our thinking. They should have, for example, different and distinct:

- *memberships* – state citizenship is determined by national governments, and most states have slightly different rules; whereas all true believers are members of the one universal church

- *beginnings* – state citizenship is granted either at birth or when certain rules are met; church membership begins only with salvation and new birth

- *functions* – the state is concerned with peace, security, and government; the church preaches and applies the gospel

- *officials* – the church is led by elders and by different types of ministers who have no status or role in the government; the state is led by politicians and judges who have no role or status in the church

- *weapons* – the state may need to go to war, but the church's weapons are exclusively spiritual

- *activities* – the church should not take on the functions of the state and the state should not interfere in the life of the church

Constantine's rebellion

In AD 312, less than three hundred years into the life of the church, the Roman emperor, Constantine, declared Christianity to be the state-religion. This defied Jesus' words in Matthew 22 and was, arguably, the single greatest set-back that the church has ever experienced.

Of course, it did not seem like that to many believers and leaders. After generations of bloody persecution, it must have seemed like a very good idea indeed.

But the gospel became a 'territorial' religion; infant baptism became universal, and everyone was deemed to be a Christian as soon as they were born within the 'Christian' state; non-Christians were persecuted; wars became 'crusades'; pastors and bishops were given a role in state affairs; the state exercised some control over church leaders; and state rulers often regarded themselves as the head of the church in their area.

Since the time of Constantine, the church and the state have related in one of three contrasting ways.

1. *hostility* – the state persecutes the church and/or the church despises the state. Church leaders either vigorously oppose the state, or they consider it irrelevant and have nothing to do with it.

2. *incorporation* – the state and the church are essentially one. The church is fully incorporated into the life of the state and is perceived to be part of the life of the nation.

    In some states, the religious leaders are more powerful; and in others, the political leaders are more influential.

Although these two ways have, historically, been most common, neither of them is consistent with Jesus' revolutionary principle. If we are to think in a deeply 'Christian' way about the relationship between the church and the state, we must pursue the third path.

3. *amicable parallelism* – the church and the state are quite distinct, and there is freedom of religion and a plurality of religions within any one state.

    The church does not claim to be – or desire, or try, to be – a state-religion; and it never talks about a 'Christian state'.

    The church supports freedom of religious conscience and freedom from religious persecution, and wants people to come voluntarily to faith in Christ.

This means that the church:

- *recognises the state* – Romans 13:1–2

- *honours the state* – Romans 13:7

- *obeys the state* – Romans 13:1

- *opposes the state when it legislates in a way which forces people to disobey God's word* – Acts 5:18–20

Romans 13:1–7 ☐

Acts 5:18–20 ☐

The church should want to be 'salt' and 'light' within the state, but it should not seek to force Christian morality upon people by state legislation. Of course, we should seek to influence and enlighten state legislation, should speak prophetically to the state, and should seek to change public opinion by our godly words and lives; but we should not use worldly methods to impose God's kingdom on people who reject God's ruler.

The church is happy for its members to participate in state affairs, but it does not value such members above others: it prays for and supports believing politicians, but only in the same way than it supports believing plumbers, believing mechanics and believing shop assistants.

This is not abandoning the state 'to the devil', as some leaders suggest. It is recognising that we are more concerned with the kingdom than the state, and that the kingdom is not established or advanced by state legislation – that was Constantine's error, and we must not seek to repeat it.

We must appreciate that the state is distinctly and directly under God. Of course, the church has a critical prophetic role in the world to pass on God's word to the state when prompted by the Spirit or asked by the state. But the church has no weapons other than prayer and the Word, and the cause of the kingdom is not served by worldly methods or pressure.

We have been called to 'render to Caesar the things that are Caesar's, and to God the things that are God's'. This principle of 'amicable parallelism' should determine how the church and state relate.

Jesus' words remind the church that we must honour the state and not usurp its rightful functions. And his words prophetically order the state not to interfere in the religious sphere. It should be clear that this little phrase has huge implications for the life and activities of both the church and the state.

These are difficult areas to work through, but the basic principle is clear: we must allow an 'amicable parallelism' and a godly distinctiveness of functioning to undergird our decisions.

PART SEVEN

belonging to the church

In the New Testament, belonging to Christ and belonging to the church cannot be separated.

Jesus' teaching about the vine, in John 15:1–8, shows that we are part of each other when we are part of him. John 15 uses the common Greek word *meno*, which means 'to live continually in' something, and is often translated as 'abide' or 'remain' or 'continue'. It is impossible for us to live continually in the true vine and not to live continually with all the other branches which are also living in the vine. It is just not possible, therefore, for anyone to abide in the true church if they are not abiding in Christ.

The various pictures of the church we have examined stress the priority of our corporate relationship with God. But four of them – body, bride, building and vine – imply that the church is much more than an association of people. They suggest that being joined, or belonging, to the church means a vital connection – an organic corporate relationship – with Christ and with each other.

This means that it is not enough to be on a church membership list or to have gone through a religious ritual. These things have meaning

John 15:1–8 ☐

only for those who are abiding in Christ and are living in a vital continuing relationship with him through his Spirit.

Many people today claim to believe in God and to be 'Christian'. Yet a considerable proportion do not attend a place of fellowship with any frequency. Sadly, even some of those who do attend do not have a relationship with Jesus. As 2 Timothy 3:5 describes, they have a form of religion but deny the life-giving power of Christ.

2 Timothy 3:5 □

CHRISTIAN INITIATION

Nominalism – being a Christian only in name – is one of the church's greatest problems right across the world. It is the fruit of Constantine's rebellion and, therefore, is especially acute in Europe – where there are more nominal Christians than in the rest of the world put together. This is one reason why we must preach the gospel in all its fullness.

We know that Jesus does offer complete salvation to all humanity, but he also commands personal and individual repentance. He does offer total forgiveness by his grace to every man, woman and child, but it is received only through personal faith.

In the New Testament, repentance and faith were held together and both had to be evidenced before a person was received into the church's life.

Joining the church, however, involves more than repentance and faith. In the New Testament, two more events occurred when believers began their new life in Christ. They were baptised in water and they were filled with the Holy Spirit.

In this way, believers began their new lives on a solid foundation and were ready to start following Christ. Through these four elements, they were fully equipped to commence a life of fellowship, discipleship and witness. So today, we need to ensure that new believers make a New Testament start to their Christian life.

We should encourage people to make a biblical beginning to their Christian and church life by taking the four basic steps of Christian initiation.

Repentance

Passages like Luke 3:8; 13:3; Acts 17:30–31 & 26:20 illustrate the importance of 'repentance'. But many modern believers are not sure what the word really means. We need to understand exactly what Jesus expected people to do when he told them to repent.

Luke 3:8 ☐
13:3 ☐
Acts 17:30–31 ☐
26:20 ☐

The Greek word *metanoia* is usually translated as 'repentance', and this literally means 'a change of mind' or 'a change of thinking'. It is formed by joining the Greek words *meta* and *noeo*. *Meta* means 'after' and implies a change (as in metamorphosis); and *noeo* means 'to think' or 'to understand'.

This suggests that repentance involves 'a change of inward understanding' rather than just 'a change in outward behaviour'. Biblical repentance means embracing God's thoughts and a brand new way of godly thinking – which lead on to God's way of living.

Repentance means a radical change in values, attitudes and outlook. It involves a change of mind and heart which leads to a radical turnabout of life. *Metanoia* means total revolution.

The New Testament call to repentance is usually best understood today as a call to 'change your understanding of God' or to 'change the way that you think about God'. We can see that this is the heart of Paul's preaching in Acts 18:22–30 which climaxes in a call to repent.

Acts 18:22–30 ☐

A changed life is the fruit of this repentance – it is the natural consequence of grasping who God really is, what he has done in Christ, and his unchanging divine values.

This means that a believer's first step in Christian initiation is stopping thinking about God in their old negative ways. Instead, they start to understand and relate to God as a Father who is full of forgiveness, grace, mercy, love and acceptance.

Because Paul wrote to established believers, he hardly mentions repentance. Romans 12:2, however, states that our behaviour should be shaped by a changed mind. Our behaviour can either be modelled on the standards, values and goals of contemporary society, or it can be transformed by a changed mind.

Romans 12:2 ☐

Romans 12:2 shows that it is this 'change of mind' which enables us to discern God's will. When we start thinking like God, we are soon pre-occupied with his will rather than with the world's ways.

Belief

Faith – or belief – is the second basic step of Christian initiation. Biblical faith is a natural progression from biblical repentance, for faith means believing – or accepting – the truth about Jesus: it is acting on our new understanding of God. We study this fully in *Living Faith*.

Becoming a Christian is beginning a relationship with Jesus Christ. Faith involves believing the truth of passages like Romans 10:8–10 which show that Jesus is the Son of God and that he is alive today because God the Father raised him from the dead.

Romans 10:8–10 ☐

Biblical belief – faith – means far more than intellectual assent. The Greek word for faith, *pistis*, is derived from the verb *peitho*, which means 'to persuade'. *Pistis*, therefore, primarily means 'to be firmly persuaded'; it is 'a strong conviction based upon hearing' – which is why Romans 10:17 insists that faith comes from hearing God's word.

Romans 10:17 ☐

But biblical faith always refers to a belief which is acted upon. Belief in Christ means trusting him completely, accepting him totally for who he is, obeying him absolutely, and thinking and acting in his ways.

In terms of Christian initiation, faith means:

- *being fully persuaded that there is nothing we can do to save ourselves – there is not even a tiny contribution that we can make*

- *being completely convinced that Christ has done everything necessary to save us*

- *receiving him willingly and becoming a child of God*

- *starting to walk with him in his ways*

John 6:35 ☐
20:30–31 ☐
Romans 8:32 ☐
Ephesians 1:3 ☐

John 6:35; 20:30–31; Romans 8:32 & Ephesians 1:3 describe the extent to which a living relationship with Jesus brings every provision of salvation that God has made available in Jesus.

Faith or belief does not create forgiveness, salvation or blessing. It is God who makes them available by grace. If we believe that God and his word are true, we can accept and apply his gifts – that is faith, relying completely on God's grace.

Too many believers think that it is *our* faith which saves us. But we are saved by *his* grace – it is all God, all his work. Our part is simply to believe that God has done everything in Jesus, to accept that there is nothing we can do, and to start living in trusting dependence on Christ. We see this in Romans 4:5 & Ephesians 2:8–10. This shows that faith is not a single act at conversion; it is a continuous life as we go on trusting God for everything.

Although belief or faith is the second step in Christian initiation, it is – like repentance – the start of an on-going, life-long process. Just as our understanding of God and his ways develops throughout our life, so too we are called to go on developing our trust and reliance in Jesus.

Baptism

Baptism in water is the third step of initiation, and it seals or ratifies a new believer's commitment to Christ. It is a formal sign or evidence of faith and, therefore, must follow faith and cannot precede it.

The biblical order is believe, and then be baptised. Of course, baptism – unlike repentance and faith – is not necessary for salvation. Instead it is a public pledge to follow Christ, an oath of allegiance to the one whom we now fully trust. We examine this more fully in Part Ten.

But for now, we must recognise that baptism is not merely something a new believer does to demonstrate their faith and repentance. The New Testament makes it clear that God himself also acts in baptism in a clear and decisive way. The water is the sign and seal of several different spiritual actions which God accomplishes. For example:

- *the Spirit is associated with baptism*: he is present at baptism; he accomplishes God's work through baptism; and he is the promised gift of baptism – John 3:5; Acts 2:38; 9:17–18; 10:47; 1 Corinthians 12:13; 2 Corinthians 1:22; Ephesians 1:13 & Titus 3:5

- *our 'sonship' is sealed in baptism* – Galatians 3:24–27

- *forgiveness and cleansing from sin are linked with baptism* – Acts 2:38; 22:16; Titus 3:5; & Hebrews 10:22

- *new birth and kingdom entry are associated with baptism* – John 3:3–5 & Titus 3:5

- *in baptism, God seals our union with the Son, our involvement in the death and burial of Christ, and our incorporation into his body* – Matthew 28:19; Acts 8:16; 19:5; Romans 6:1–11; 1 Corinthians 12:13 & Galatians 3:27

Romans 4:5 ☐

Ephesians 2:8–10 ☐

Acts 2:38 ☐
9:17–18 ☐
10:47 ☐

1 Corinthians 12:13 ☐

2 Corinthians 1:22 ☐

Ephesians 1:13 ☐

Titus 3:5 ☐

Matthew 28:19 ☐

Acts 8:16 ☐
19:5 ☐

Romans 6:1–11 ☐

1 Corinthians 12:13 ☐

Galatians 3:27 ☐

These blessings do not come *from* baptism; they are confirmed by God *through* baptism. Although they are pledged by him at baptism, they are enjoyed only through our obedient faith *following* baptism. Romans 6:1–11 makes this clear.

The blessings of baptism – the third step of initiation – do not operate automatically. Rather, baptism is God's promise that he has secured these blessings for a new believer. Baptism looks back to God's work on the cross and forward to a brand new life of faith.

Receiving the Spirit

The fourth and final step of initiation equips a believer for the new life of faith in the church. The New Testament uses several different phrases to describe receiving the Spirit – filled with the Spirit, baptised in the Spirit, anointed with the Spirit, and sealed with the Spirit.

Whichever expression is used, the New Testament shows that the Holy Spirit is God's crowning seal – or completion – of the conversion process. He comes to take up grand residence in the life of a believer *and* to equip us for effective service in partnership with himself.

Joel 2:28–29 ☐

Ezekiel 36:25–27 ☐

The Spirit was at work like this in the Old Testament in the lives of the prophets: he both indwelt and empowered them. Joel 2:28–29 & Ezekiel 36:25–27 prophesied that the time would come when the Spirit would be freely available to indwell and empower *all* believers.

John 14:16–23 ☐

2 Corinthians 4:17–18 ☐

In John 14:16–23, Jesus taught that the Spirit would be sent to help all believers when he had returned to heaven. And 2 Corinthians 4:17–18 shows that the chief work of the Spirit is to bring 'the presence' *and* 'the activity' of Christ into the life of every believer.

Romans 8:9 ☐

Of course, Romans 8:9 makes it plain that every Christian has the Spirit working in them from the time of new birth. But the anointing with, or baptism in, the Spirit is the special moment when God stamps his mark of ownership on believers by sealing them with his Spirit.

Luke 24:49 ☐

Acts 1:8 ☐
10:44–45 ☐
11:15–17 ☐
19:2–6 ☐

Belonging to Christ also means being equipped by the Spirit for effective service. This equipping is not automatic, and is additional to the Spirit's coming at the new birth. Luke 24:49; Acts 1:8; 10:44–45; 11:15–17 & 19:2–6 demonstrate that equipping for effective service is a definite, conscious experience which is accompanied by spiritual phenomena.

Acts 8:14–17; 9:17 & 19:2 suggest that the New Testament church ensured that every believer had fully received the Spirit so that they could be effective witnesses for Christ.

Acts 8:14–17 ☐
9:17 ☐
19:2 ☐

Five scriptural principles are associated with this equipping.

1. The purpose of receiving the Spirit is empowering for service – Luke 24:49; John 16:7–15 & Acts 1:8. The Spirit is not given for selfish or entertaining purposes, but to enable the church to reach the lost and fulfil its God-given charge.

Luke 24:49 ☐

John 16:7–15 ☐

Acts 1:8 ☐
2:38–39 ☐

2. The empowering or equipping is for everyone and not just a few special Christians. It is for every member of the church – Acts 2:38–39. It is for 'as many as the Lord our God will call', so it is not restricted to the New Testament era.

3. The equipping follows faith. In every scriptural example, those who were filled with the Spirit had *already* believed. This shows that the empowering is not given automatically at new birth. We can see that the early church leaders made sure every new believer sought the Spirit, and they prayed with them to receive the Spirit – Acts 8:14–17; 9:17; 19:2–6; Ephesians 1:13.

Acts 8:14–17 ☐
9:17 ☐
19:2–6 ☐

Ephesians 1:13 ☐

4. The equipping is a free gift. The Spirit was poured out at Pentecost and is now freely available to the church. The Spirit is a gift from God for every believer, not a reward for those who are outstandingly holy or talented – Galatians 3:2, 13–14.

Galatians 3:2 ☐
3:13–14 ☐

5. The equipping is evidenced by prophetic speech – especially by speaking in tongues. As 1 Samuel 10:10–11; 19:20–24 & Numbers 11:16–30 show that people prophesied in the Old Testament when the Spirit came upon them, it should not surprise us that people spoke prophetically when they were empowered by the Spirit in the New Testament – Luke 1:41–45, 67; Acts 2:4; 10:44–47; 19:5–6.

1 Samuel
10:10–11 ☐
19:20–24 ☐

Numbers
11:16–30 ☐

Luke 1:41–45 ☐
1:67 ☐

Acts 2:4 ☐
10:44–47 ☐
19:5–6 ☐

Tongues is a new form of prophetic speech for the new era of the Holy Spirit, but all forms of prophetic speech in the New Testament are for praising God or for powerful witness to the risen Lord.

Some people want to know whether they will go to heaven if they have not been baptised, or have not been empowered with the Spirit. The Bible makes it plain that we are saved by grace through faith alone. Baptism and receiving the Spirit are not conditions for entering God's heaven, but they are pre-requisites for enjoying the promises and benefits of eternal life in this life.

Joining Christ is not merely about getting a 'ticket to heaven'. It means being equipped to live with and for Jesus on earth, being his body, doing his work with his effectiveness, revealing his glory to the nations, fighting his enemies, and all the other things we have seen. God wants us to receive everything he has for us and not to be content with the minimum.

CHURCH COMMITMENT

We have seen that we become members of the church by believing in Jesus. Every true believer is automatically a member of the universal church. But we also know that our membership of the universal church must be expressed through membership of a local, household church. Local church commitment is a basic requirement for every Christian.

It is obvious that there can be no real life in the church without commitment – the body cannot function without committed and clearly recognised members.

Ephesians 4:11–12 ☐

Church members are a work force. In Ephesians 4:11–12, church leaders are called to knit the members together and equip them for the work of ministry. This is possible only when it is clear who is committed to each local expression of the church.

Acts 1:15 ☐
2:1 ☐
2:44 ☐
2:47 ☐

The Greek phrase in the New Testament for church membership seems to be *epi to auto*. This first appears in Acts 1:15, 'the number of believers together – *epi to auto* – was....' and implies a formally constituted body. It also appears in Acts 2:1; 2:44; & 2:47.

Some leaders suggest that churches in the New Testament had no structure, and that the Holy Spirit blesses only where there is no organisation to restrict him. But people knew when they were joining a New Testament church and they knew when they were leaving – as in 1 Corinthians 5:2. They did certain things when they were gathered together in the church; they were committed to each other; and they came together to do certain tasks.

1 Corinthians 5:2 ☐

Each fellowship was formally expressed and structured – they were not loose collections of individuals. Their members were part of a body and were held together by spiritual bonds in a cross-forged relationship. Each household fellowship was part of the one body, relating in love and commitment to the other local expressions of the one body.

The 'body' teaching in Ephesians 4:15–16 & Colossians 2:18–19 shows that Christian commitment is indistinguishable from church commitment. Belonging to Christ means being in union with – being joined to – one body. Holding on to the head means being committed in a functioning, interdependent relationship with all the other members of the body in the local church.

Ephesians
4:15–16 ☐

Colossians
2:18–19 ☐

If we do not 'abide' in a local fellowship, we are in danger of spiritually withering away. And if any local fellowship is not committed to its neighbouring congregations, it too is in danger of damaging the one body. No individual, and no congregation, can live the Christian life in isolation: there must be genuine commitment to the one body at *every* level.

We see, in the life of both Jesus and the early church, that early believers worked their commitment out in four complementary ways. Until recently, however, most church leaders have focused on these two:

- *an individual response to Christ*

- *the congregation grouping*

Believers have been expected to be committed personally to Christ and also to be part of a local congregation which exists independently of other local congregations. We must appreciate that believers in the early church expressed their commitment in a greater variety of ways.

Companion

We know from John 19:26 & 21:20 that the apostle John was particularly close to Jesus. He was 'the beloved disciple'. Although Jesus had his own private relationship with his Father, and had relationships with the twelve and the wider group of disciples, he also had a special companion in John.

John 19:26 ☐
21:20 ☐

Matthew 10:1–5 describes Jesus commissioning the apostles for ministry, and lists them in pairs. When they went out to minister, they did not go alone. They each had a particular companion.

Matthew 10:1–5 ☐

Luke 10:1 records that Jesus also sent out a wider group of seventy disciples in pairs, and Acts 12:25 & 16:25 illustrate how Paul had a series of close companions. Even in Revelation 11, there are two witnesses rather than one or a larger number.

The companionship principle is founded on the relationships which eternally exist within the Godhead. Throughout the Scriptures we see repeated references to 'the Father and the Son' and 'the Word and the Spirit'. Partnership, not individualism, is at the heart of our faith.

Genesis 1:26–27 points to the essential corporate nature of humanity, and makes it plain that this is God's image. And Genesis 2:18 shows the importance God gives to human companionship. Naturally, marriage is the most obvious way of expressing this principle, but we must not restrict companionship within the church to the home.

We can see the companion dimension of church life in the Old Testament, in pairs like Moses and Aaron, David and Jonathan, Elijah and Elisha, Ruth and Naomi, Haggai and Zerubbabel, Joshua and Zechariah, Ezra and Nehemiah. Many of these people were also married, but their companionship in God went beyond their spouses.

With the exception of Elijah and Elisha, who were both prophets, the other Old Testament companions involved people with different callings under God. Their respective ministries were tremendously enhanced by their companionship, and we have much to learn from their relationships.

This dimension has been largely overlooked in church life. There have been few men who have consistently ministered with a particularly close companion; but many of those who have – like Charles and John Wesley, Nikolaus Zinzendorf and August Spangenberg, and Dwight Moody and Ira Sankey – have been outstandingly blessed by God.

The principle of companionship undergirded the astonishing Moravian missionary movement which was pioneered by Zinzendorf and Spangenberg: between 1732 and 1757, they sent over fifty pairs of missionaries all over the world from the tiny village of Herrnhut in Saxony.

John Wesley was greatly affected by the Moravians, and he ensured that his converts were linked with a spiritual companion who could guide their discipleship.

Other preachers of his day, like Whitfield, may have seen more converts than Wesley, but the principle of companionship ensured that Wesley's legacy to the church was stronger and longer-lasting.

If we are serious about understanding the church in a biblical way, we will find ways of developing and encouraging true companionship within the church – but not to the exclusion of other commitments.

Cell

It is instructive that Jesus carefully chose a small group of twelve disciples whom he taught in a particularly intimate way. We also see, in Acts, that Paul usually drew a small team around himself who learnt from him and ministered with him. There was no fixed number for this group but it seems to have varied between three and twelve.

Acts 20:4 ☐

27:2 ☐

There are different dynamics in a group of this size. People can know each other well, can care practically for each other, can know that they belong and have a special role. Groups of this size seem to have been the New Testament leadership pattern for training, as everyone can develop their own part in Christ's ministry in a secure way.

Acts 6:1–7 ☐

Much of the scriptural teaching about the church is 'do this or that to one another'. All these different exhortations can be worked out best in a small group of this size.

Small cell groups have commonly been a feature of the church at times of great growth and blessing. For example, this dimension of church life was fundamental to the early preaching monks who first converted Europe.

And Zinzendorf, who believed that 'there can be no Christianity without community', ensured that his companions gathered in small groups to pray together, to care for each other, and to learn from each other. These cells were at the heart of Moravian missions and church-planting. Wesley then developed the Moravian cells into his 'class-system', which facilitated the worship and discipleship of his converts in small groups of no more than ten believers.

Many modern churches have established cell groups in recent years. But too many of these have been much bigger than twelve and have been rather 'meeting' orientated. With few contemporary cell-groups to learn from, church leaders in the seventies and eighties tended to develop mini mid-week services – miniature congregations – rather than action, training and caring groups which express *ekklesia* and *koinonia* in a locality and have featured in the church in the past.

Congregation

Once a group is larger than twelve it is hard for everyone to know each other equally well. In groups from twelve to about 200, there remains a level of intimacy and everybody can know each other's name and participate in some way. Groups of this size can be seen in Luke 10:1–20 and Acts 1:1, and most New Testament churches would have begun at this level.

Luke 10:1–20 ☐

Acts 1:1 ☐

More can be done with congregation size groups. They are large enough to be a visible presence in the local community, but small enough for individuals to contribute in worship along the lines of 1 Corinthians 14:26.

1 Corinthians
14:26 ☐

Since the Reformation, most Protestant church leaders have concentrated almost exclusively on the congregational dimension. This narrow focus has tended to be a barrier to church growth, to training and releasing believers in ministry, and to discipling new converts.

Celebration

Meetings inevitably become spectator orientated when groups are larger than 200, but the New Testament contains several examples of very large groups of people gathering to hear God's word – these are community celebrations.

Acts 2:41 ☐
4:4 ☐

Large gatherings – from 200 to several thousand – have a special dynamic which establishes a strong corporate identity – even though very few believers can take part publicly. People are encouraged by feeling part of a larger whole, but we must remember that 'church' is much more than celebration.

Jesus – our example in all things – was committed to intimate companionship with John, to twelve apostles, to the large group of disciples from whom the seventy were selected, and to the crowds of thousands who wanted to hear him speak. Jesus moved with ease between all these groups, and we can see that the early church followed his example.

There is a dynamic tension in holding these complementary commitments together – every believer feels more comfortable in one group and less comfortable in another. But we do need to redress some of our present imbalances so that we develop a full experience and practice of the church.

If we want to move towards a biblical church, it is important that we rediscover these four layers of commitment – both as individuals and as congregations. Without this strong commitment, the church will remain weak and divided and the world will stay unreached and unconvinced.

PART EIGHT

leadership in the church

We have seen that the New Testament considers the church to be an organism rather than an organisation. According to the Oxford English dictionary, an organism is 'an organised body consisting of mutually connected and dependent parts constituted to share a common life'.

This means that the church can function effectively only when every expression of the universal church (all companions, cells, congregations and celebrations; all household and local churches) is interdependent and co-dependent on Christ.

It also means that the church can function effectively only when it has some sort of structure and leadership. In the Old Testament, God's glory generally came where there was a structure like the Temple and Tabernacle. And every New Testament picture of the church involves a structure, and most imply some degree of leadership and government.

Every picture of the church is also corporate and demands some sort of organisation. Bricks need to be touching and bonded together; flesh must be attached to muscle and bone; nations need good government; buildings need careful design and solid structures; armies must have a gifted leadership – or they are destined to defeat.

1 Corinthians
        12:18 ☐

Ephesians 4:16 ☐

John 15:1–8 ☐

Before examining these things we need to remind ourselves of three important biblical principles:

- *every member of the body of Christ is ordered of God –* 1 Corinthians 12:18

- *every member of the body is mutually connected, dependent, joined and held together –* Ephesians 4:16

- *every member of the body shares the common life of Christ, the head –* John 15:1–8

And we need to remember the three principles of Greek city assemblies which lie behind the *ekklesia* picture:

- *every* ekklesia *had unlimited powers:* it elected and dismissed leaders, directed military operations, raised and allocated funds, and assigned people to different tasks

- *every* ekklesia *commenced with prayer and sacrifice*

- *every* ekklesia *treated all its citizens as equals:* all free citizens had equal rights and duties – no one member was more important than any other

CHURCH STRUCTURE

No expression of the church can function without a structure. If we started a community church today, we would need to make arrangements for meetings and taking decisions. We would have to learn from the Scriptures and the Spirit how to express our church life.

The New Testament does not provide us with a blueprint for a perfect church structure and an ideal organisation. It does, however, offer several important principles. These need to be applied in any church which is serious about moving towards a more biblical pattern.

United yet diverse

The 'body' metaphor emphasises that there are many different members within the church who each have a quite different function.

Any and every church structure must seek to express both the body's unity of purpose and also its diversity of function.

It is a basic principle of the church that 'there is only one church, but there are very many gifts'. This must be worked out practically in every church which is trying to follow biblical principles. Somehow, churches must be co-ordinated and organised whilst ensuring that there is ample room for a wide variety of expressions of Christ's ministry.

Equal yet distinct

The principle of equality which is inherent in the Greek idea of *ekklesia* is also stressed in the New Testament. 1 Corinthians 12:22–26 & James 2:1–4 make it plain that 'status' has no place in the church.

1 Corinthians
  12:22–26 ☐

James 2:1–4 ☐

Just as those parts of the human body which are not presentable are given greater honour, so in the church body those members who appear less important must be honoured, valued and esteemed.

We are all equal in the sight of God, and all equal in his body, so we must not adopt structures which classify some people as more important than others. Those who have been entrusted with leadership gifts may be more prominent and have greater responsibilities, but they are not superior or more important than the rest of the body.

Of course, we must be as well managed as the best business, but our foundation attitude must be one of equal worth and equal value.

There should also be a distinction of function within the equality. A Greek *ekklesia* appointed a few members to be generals, others to be magistrates, and sent some citizens out from the city on special tasks. And Ephesians 4:11–13 & 1 Corinthians 12 4–11 show that there is one Spirit but many gifts – which he distributes at will.

Ephesians
  4:11–13 ☐

1 Corinthians
  12 4–11 ☐

There is always a temptation to ascribe too much importance to one gift, or to consider one function to be over-important. 1 Corinthians 12:28–31 does show that prophecy is a higher gift, but we must always apply the 1 Corinthians 13:13 principle.

  12:28–31 ☐
  13:13 ☐

Total membership involvement

Many modern churches are led by a professional elite. Their members think that they should support an omni-competent minister who is supposed to do everything on their behalf. In recent years, however, the Spirit has led the church into the biblical truth that ministry belongs to all the saints.

Ephesians 4:11–12 □

Ephesians 4:11–12 explains that leaders are meant to equip the saints for the work of ministry: they are not supposed to do it all for them. The growth and health of the body depends on each part functioning to capacity. Churches need structures which encourage this vital truth.

Fully flexible

It is self evident that dead bodies do not grow and change. Living organisms are always on the move. In Luke 5:37–39, Jesus taught that new wine needs new wineskins. In those days, unfermented wine was put into bags made from animal skins. The wine expanded as it fermented, and the skins were flexible enough to accommodate it.

Luke 5:37–39 □

When the wine had been used, the old skin could not be re-used because it had lost its pliability – unless it was thoroughly soaked to restore its elasticity.

In the same way, church structures cannot contain the new life and growth of the Spirit when they are rigid and inflexible. The only way that church structures can function effectively is by being flexible enough to allow constant renewing by the Spirit.

CHURCH GOVERNMENT

No 'nation', 'army', 'city', 'family' or church can function without government. Throughout history the church has never settled on one system of government, as the New Testament does not lay down rigid rules. Instead, the Scriptures offer guidelines for us to apply with the Spirit's help.

We know that Christ is the head of the church, so every expression of *ekklesia* is under his government. No single human system can perfectly reproduce Christ's rule. He may express his rule through one individual, a few, or all his people.

God in his sovereignty is free to express his will however he chooses. It is simply up to us to listen to him as carefully as we can.

Traditionally the church has used one of four main systems of church government.

Episcopalian

In the Church of England, every parish has a church, over every church is a minister, and over every minister is a bishop. This is a hierarchical system, but it can work well when the bishops and ministers are full of God's love and passion. At its best, it guarantees that all pastors are themselves pastored properly.

Presbyterian

This is rule by a small group of elders or presbyters who have been chosen or elected by some system. It works well when the elders are in agreement and have jointly heard God's will. Its great advantage is that it is clear to all who governs the local church.

Congregational

This is democratic rule by the majority of the congregation. This works well when a whole congregation is moved by God's power and there is a clear consensus about his will. Ideally, this reveals the important truth that Christ is in the whole body, and not just an elite. But the majority is not always right – as we see in Numbers 13:1–14:10.

Numbers
13:1–14:10 ☐

Apostolic

This is rule by one strong leader who calls people to follow him and do the work of God. Again, this works well when the leader has been envisioned and anointed by God. Its strength is that there is always a clear and agreed vision. But who pastors the leader? And who takes over when he moves on?

Clearly no system of church government is perfect, and history shows that God will use any of them. We must simply try to recognise his voice – whether in the congregation, an outside ministry, an individual or a group of elders. Six basic scriptural principles need to be kept in mind whenever church government is considered.

1.   Christ is the one and only head. He is the ultimate church leader.

2.   There are a variety of leadership gifts which are not vested in one omni-competent individual.

3.   Christ is himself present in all the members – each member can hear God for themselves through the Spirit.

4.   Jesus came not to be served but to serve, and he set an example of foot-washing for his under-leaders to follow. Authoritarian or coercive patterns of government should be absent.

5.   Every expression of the church has integrity and is a valid unit.

6.   Every expression of the church should be interdependent and co-dependent with all other local expressions – and in some relationship with wider expressions of the world-wide body.

CHURCH LEADERSHIP

No church can function without leaders and leadership, and Jesus is the leader of his church. He governs and directs the church through his word and through his Spirit. Whatever our role in the church, we have to submit to Christ's headship.

Ephesians 5:21 □

When we submit to Christ we are submitting to each other, as all are equally joined to Christ. Ephesians 5:21 teaches that we all are subject to each other – because we acknowledge Christ in each other. This means that leadership is not a few ruling the many, but all serving each other in a variety of ways – of which leadership is only one.

1.   Local leadership

The New Testament church appears to have had a basic two-fold leadership pattern which involved elders and deacons.

Elders and overseers

The New Testament refers to both *episkopos* and *presbuteros*. *Episkopos* comes from *epi*, 'over', and *skopea*, 'to look', and literally means an 'overseer'. It is often translated into English as 'bishop', and is used in Acts 20:28; Philippians 1:1; 1 Timothy 3:2; Titus 1:7 & 1 Peter 2:25.

Presbuteros means 'elder' and is another word for the same person as 'overseer' or 'bishop'. We see this in Acts 20:17–28, where Paul summons the *presbuteros* of the church at Ephesus and then calls them *episkopos*.

The term 'elder' indicates the mature, spiritual experience and understanding of the particular leaders, and the words 'overseer' or 'bishop' point to the work that they do: it is the 'elders' who 'oversee' or 'bishop' the saints – we see this in 1 Peter 5:1–2.

Acts 14:23; 20:17; Philippians 1:1; Titus 1:5 & James 5:14 show that a small group of overseers or elders should be appointed in every church. The only passages which refer to a single bishop either point to Christ – 1 Peter 2:25 – or describe what each individual *episkopos* should be like, as in 1 Timothy 3:1.

1 Timothy 3:1–7 & Titus 1:5–9 list the qualities which every single elder or bishop should possess.

And Acts 11:30; 15:4–6, 23; 16:4; 1 Timothy 4:14; 5:17; James 5:14 & 1 Peter 5:2 show that elders, overseers, bishops were involved in:

- *visiting and healing the sick*

- *teaching God's word and Christian doctrine*

- *receiving gifts on behalf of the community*

- *recognising and laying hands on gifted members*

- *ruling and overseeing the local congregation*

- *taking part in wider church councils*

Most elders seem to have been of equal rank and to have acted corporately, as in 1 Timothy 4:14 where the body of elders ordained Timothy. Acts 15:5–21, however, indicates that James was the senior elder in Jerusalem – a 'first among equals' with a presiding role.

We can say that elders are called to 'guard, guide and graze'. That is to guard the flock from the enemy, to guide the people along the ways of God, and to graze the members by teaching and preaching.

Deacons

Deacons were called and equipped to assist the elders in all the practical and serving details so that the elders could apply themselves fully to the work of spiritual oversight.

The Greek word *diakonos* means 'servant' and is often used in the New Testament for waiting at tables – for example, Mark 1:31 & Luke 10:40. Interestingly, Jesus introduces himself as 'The Deacon' in Luke 22:26 in the context of waiting at table.

Diakanos is also used in relation to general, practical ministry in Romans 15:25 & 2 Corinthians 8:4, and to those who help Paul practically in Acts 19:22; Philemon 13; Colossians 4:7 & Ephesians 6:21. We examine this word in Part One of *Ministry in the Spirit*.

In Romans 12:7 & 1 Peter 4:11, 'serving', *diakonia*, is named as a special gift from God. It is on a par with prophecy and ruling, and is meant to be exercised by those who have received this gift from God.

It is usually inferred that the Spirit-filled men of Acts 6 were the first deacons – though they are not named as such. They had the responsibility of administering the widows' fund, and of releasing the apostles for the ministry of the Word.

1 Timothy 3:8–11 describes the character of deacons, and 1 Timothy 3:11 seems to mention female deacons (or deaconesses): certainly Phoebe is named as a deaconess in Romans 16:1.

We must remember that titles are not important, what matters is that the biblical leadership functions are being fulfilled. Local churches need not call their leaders 'elders' and 'deacons', so long as there is an identifiable corporate leadership doing these jobs.

2.   Trans-local leadership

Each New Testament local church had its own leadership and was responsible directly to the head of the church, to Jesus.

In Revelation, there is a different message from the head to each church in Asia Minor. Christ had a specific word for each church, but these messages were to be heard by all the other churches; which is why Jesus says, 'hear what the Spirit says to the *churches*' in Revelation 2:7, 11, 17, 29; 3:6, 13, 22.

Margin references:

Mark 1:31 ☐
Luke 10:40 ☐
   22:26 ☐

Romans 15:25 ☐
2 Corinthians 8:4 ☐
Acts 19:22 ☐
Philemon 13 ☐
Colossians 4:7 ☐
Ephesians 6:21 ☐
Romans 12:7 ☐
1 Peter 4:11 ☐
Acts 6 ☐
1 Timothy 3:8–11 ☐
Romans 16:1 ☐

Revelation 2:7 ☐
   2:11 ☐
   2:17 ☐
   2:29 ☐
   3:6 ☐
   3:13 ☐
   3:22 ☐

This re-enforces the fact that every local church is only one expression of the body. We cannot break away from each other; there must be relationship between churches.

One of the best ways of maintaining these relationships is by recognising ministries at a trans-local level. This means that we receive ministries which are God's gift to the whole body even though they are based in a different expression of the church – even another country. This is precisely what we see in Revelation, where each Asian church had its own local leadership, but recognised and benefited from John's wider ministry.

Obviously, all the ministries listed in Ephesians 4:11 should be rooted in local churches where they should work alongside the elders, as in Acts 15:6, 22–23. The Ephesians 4:11 ministries, however, also seem to have a trans-local function.

Biblical local churches should be overseen, or 'bishopped', by elders – some of whom will also probably be apostles, prophets, evangelists, pastors and teachers. Their eldership is a purely local ministry.

Within the church, however, those with an Ephesians 4:11 gifting can express their ministry both through their local church and also beyond it – in other local churches where they are welcomed by the elders and, like Paul in Acts 21:17–25, they submit to those elders.

Apostles

The Greek word *apostolos*, 'apostle', is derived from *apo*, 'from', and *stello*, 'to send'. It literally means 'one who is sent forth', so 'apostles' are those who are sent or commissioned.

In the New Testament there are at least three types of apostles:

- *Jesus Christ*, who was sent from God – Hebrews 3:1; John 17:3

- *foundation apostles*, who were sent from Jesus – Luke 6:13; 9:10

- *general apostles*, who were sent from the head of the church via his under-leaders – Acts 14:4; Romans 16:7; 2 Corinthians 8:23; Philippians 2:25; 1 Thessalonians 2:6

Foundation apostles were chosen by Jesus as special eye witnesses who had been with him from the start. They had unique and unrepeatable qualifications. They had special authority to witness

Ephesians 4:11 ☐

Acts 15:6 ☐
15:22–23 ☐

Acts 21:17–25 ☐

Hebrews 3:1 ☐

John 17:3 ☐

Luke 6:13 ☐
9:10 ☐

Acts 14:4 ☐

Romans 16:7 ☐

2 Corinthians
8:23 ☐

Philippians 2:25 ☐

1 Thessalonians
2:6 ☐

and pass on Christ's teaching. Obviously they belonged only to the first generation of believers.

Some leaders teach that foundation apostles were the only apostles. But the New Testament also names Barnabas, Andronicus and Junias (probably a woman) as apostles. And Ephesians 4:11 indicates that all the giftings are to build up the church *until* it is fully mature. Clearly, this will not be attained until Jesus returns.

We can say, therefore, that apostles are necessary for building and equipping the saints in every age and place until the end of time.

The first apostles were sent ahead of Jesus to the places he would be visiting, and apostles are always pioneers who are sent ahead to spearhead the work of the gospel.

The Scriptures show that apostles have several distinctive characteristics:

1.   *Fatherhood*

1 Corinthians 4:15 suggests that spiritual fatherhood is at the heart of apostolic ministry. This speaks of wise, life-giving leadership, of nurture and protection, and of the gifting to get things started. 1 Corinthians 3:10 shows that apostles establish God's work and build up the church. They inspire and motivate others with God's vision

2.   *Authority*

2 Corinthians 10:8 suggests that apostles have authority in the Spirit to see God's vision fulfilled, but we must note that this is not authority *over* churches. Paul supported and encouraged churches, he confronted their sins and errors, but he never commanded or directed them – that is the task of local elders.

3.   *Signs and wonders*

2 Corinthians 12:12 establishes that the ministry of the miraculous is a vital characteristic of apostles.

4.   *Raising leaders and releasing giftings*

Paul always travelled and ministered in teams, and was deeply involved in training and releasing ministries. We see this in 2 Timothy 2:2 & Romans 1:11–12.

Sidebar references:

Ephesians 4:11 ☐

1 Corinthians 4:15 ☐

1 Corinthians 3:10 ☐

2 Corinthians 10:8 ☐

2 Corinthians 12:12 ☐

2 Timothy 2:2 ☐

Romans 1:11–12 ☐

5. *Structuring and strengthening church life*

Acts 14:23 & 15:41 describe apostles appointing local leaders in newly established churches and visiting churches to strengthen them.

Acts 14:23 ☐
15:41 ☐

6. *Precise calling*

2 Corinthians 10:13 shows that Paul was called to a precise area. Apostles are not just 'sent', they are sent to specific places or people groups.

2 Corinthians 10:13 ☐

Prophets

The Greek word *prophetes*, 'prophet', comes from *pro*, 'forth', and *phemi*, 'to speak'. It literally means 'one who speaks forth' and describes someone who speaks God's words and reveals his thoughts.

Prophets are called to live in close communion with God. They enter his presence to hear his thoughts, and emerge to preach, encourage and explain what God is doing, or to challenge the standards and behaviour of the church and the world.

Ideally, prophets pass on only what God is thinking and doing, and do not taint the message with their own opinions and cultural values.

In the New Testament, there appear to be two types of prophets:

Acts 13:1 ☐

1 Corinthians
12:10 ☐
12:28 ☐
13:1 ☐
13:8–9 ☐
14:1–6 ☐
14:29–39 ☐

- *those who functioned only within a local church* – where all people were always encouraged to seek God for prophecy, Acts 13:1; 1 Corinthians 12:10, 28; 13:1, 8–9; 14:1–6, 29–39

- *those who were recognised more widely and functioned trans-locally*, Acts 11:27–28; 21:10–11: these are the prophets referred to in Ephesians 4:11

Acts 11:27–28 ☐
21:10–11 ☐

The New Testament ministry of prophet involved seven principles:

1. It was officially recognised. Men or women whom a local church recognised over a period of time as regularly receiving and passing on prophecies were identified as prophets. They were not appointed to a position; they were recognised when they had proved that they had a share in Christ's prophetic ministry.

2. Their ministry involved factual revelation – Acts 11:27–30; 13:1–3.

Acts 11:27–30 ☐
13:1–3 ☐

3. They spoke by the inspiration of the Holy Spirit – Acts 11:27.

4. They were not infallible. Agabus' prophecy in Acts 21:10 was broadly accurate, but some of the details did not occur exactly as he had prophesied. This did not nullify the thrust of his message – which was true. Even so, Paul did not act on the message; instead he used it to prepare himself for the coming ordeal.

This shows that we have a serious duty to 'judge' prophecy, as in 1 Corinthians 14:29–32. The Greek word *diakrisis*, 'judge' or 'discern' means 'to separate', and shows that the 'others' (the Greek word *allos* refers to the other prophets) do not accept or reject the entire message, instead they separate out the human dross and point to the divine kernel.

5. They predicted the future – Acts 11:27–30.

6. They gave direction for ministry which confirmed what people already knew – Acts 13:11–3; 1 Timothy 1:18, 4:14; 2 Timothy 1:6.

7. They pointed to what God was doing, as in Acts 11:27–30. Agabus did not demand a human response; he simply warned of a coming famine and left it to the people to respond as they were led. The trans-local prophet passed on God's word, and the local leaders decided how the prophecy should be acted upon.

Evangelists

The Greek word *euangelistes*, 'evangelist', comes from *eu*, 'well' and *angelos*, 'messenger' and means 'one who brings good news'.

The verb *euangelizo*, which means 'to announce the good news', is very common in the New Testament, but the title *euangelistes* appears only three times.

- *Timothy is urged to do the work of an evangelist* – 2 Timothy 4:5

- *Philip is described as 'the evangelist'* – Acts 21:8

- *the office is listed as a special gift to the church* – Ephesians 4:11

Although all Christians are called 'to announce the good news', there are those with a special gifting in evangelism. The only evangelists mentioned in the New Testament, Philip and Timothy, both had local and trans-local ministries. Acts describes Philip's travels in Samaria before settling in Caesarea. And Timothy travelled with Paul before settling in Ephesus.

Pastors

The Greek word *poimen* literally means 'a shepherd', and describes someone who cares for animals and feeds them. It is used metaphorically of Christian 'pastors' to identify those who tend the flock of God.

Jesus is the good Shepherd, and he continues to care for his sheep through 'under shepherds' – through the pastors he gives to his church.

Throughout the Scriptures, 'shepherd' leadership is constantly revealed as God's heart for his people. We see this, for example, in Genesis 48:15; 49:24; Psalm 23:1; 28:9; 78:70–72; Isaiah 40:11; Ezekiel 34:23–24; Matthew 2:6; 9:36; John 10:11; 21:16–17; Acts 20:28–31; 1 Peter 5:1–4.

Genesis 48:15 ☐
49:24 ☐

Psalm 23:1 ☐
28:9 ☐
78:70–72 ☐

Isaiah 40:11 ☐

Ezekiel 34:23–24 ☐

Matthew 2:6 ☐
9:36 ☐

John 10:11 ☐
21:16–17 ☐

Acts 20:28–31 ☐

1 Peter 5:1–4 ☐

Pastors have very wide responsibilities for their flock:

- *gathering* – they know the sheep, gather them together and keep them together as a flock

- *guarding* – they keep watch over God's flock with their lives

- *guiding* – they lead the sheep from the front to good pastures

- *grazing* – they make sure that the sheep are well fed

- *praying* – they stay alert and keep on praying for all the saints

- *listening* – they give the sheep individual attention; they take James 1:19 seriously, and learn to listen and understand others

James 1:19 ☐

- *admonishing* – they correct and admonish, speaking the truth in love so that each person can be presented perfect in Christ

- *caring* – they apply 1 John 3:16–18 & James 2:15–18 and care practically for any needy sheep

1 John 3:16–18 ☐

James 2:15–18 ☐

- *healing* – they heal their sick sheep are ensure that healing is an integral part of the life of the flock

- *counselling* – they bear their sheep's burdens by giving them God's words in a sensitive, creative and caring manner

- *supporting* – they accept spiritual responsibility for the sheep, and seek to support, encourage and build them up

Teachers

Ephesians 4:11 also states that Christ gives 'teachers' to the church. The Greek word *didaskalos*, 'teacher' means 'to give instruction' or 'to instruct'.

God gifts certain people with the ability to grasp biblical truths and communicate an understanding of them – practically, regularly and systematically – to all the saints. 2 Timothy 3:16–17 suggests that teachers should use the Scriptures to:

2 Timothy
    3:16–17 ☐

- *teach us what God requires*

- *rebuke us when we fall short*

- *correct us and show us how to get right again*

- *train us to stay on the right path*

It is teachers who edify believers by instructing them in the ways and attitudes of God. And it is teachers who are used by the Spirit to shape the lives of Christians into the image of Christ.

Matthew 28:20 ☐

Acts 2:42 ☐

1 Timothy 5:17 ☐

Acts 20:28 ☐

Romans 12:7 ☐

We see the important role of teaching in the church in Matthew 28:20; Acts 2:42; 1 Timothy 5:17; Acts 20:28 and Romans 12:7.

Pastors and teachers perform an indispensable function. They build on the foundations laid down by apostles, prophets and evangelists. Many of them stay in one place, often for many years, caring for the church. They establish it on scriptural foundations, and emphasise its essential unity with all believers down the centuries, through the traditions, and across the world.

Pastors and teachers also have a vital trans-local function. Those with a special gifting in teaching are often called to travel widely – especially to teach other teachers. And those with a special pastoral gifting can offer pastoral help to those pastors and leaders who are not themselves being pastored because of their church's government structure.

Ephesians 4:12 ☐

Ephesians 4:12 shows that all these ministries were given by Jesus to prepare the whole church for service. And the Greek word he uses, *diakonia*, means practical, menial, foot-washing, table-waiting service. Each individual believer is meant to serve God, other disciples and the world. But the different categories of leaders are meant to ensure that the church as a whole is characterised by this sort of humble service.

PART NINE

the functioning church

We have seen, in Ephesians 3, that Christ has given his church the basic responsibility of revealing God's glory (his nature, wisdom, beauty, authority and presence) to all the nations in the earthly world *and* to the principalities and powers in the heavenly places.

We have noted Jesus' words in Matthew 16:18, and established that the church he builds will be characterised by an offensive, warlike nature. And we have examined Christ's prayer in John 17, and grasped that his church is meant to be guided by his word, filled with his joy, united in his love, and sent into his world so that people will believe.

We have looked at the idea of *qahal* in the Old Testament, and have realised this suggests that Christ's *ekklesia* has also been gathered together to praise God, to fight God's enemies, and to reveal God's glory 'in the sight of the world' by the way that it lives and loves.

We have studied *ekklesia* and *koinonia*, and have recognised that we have been gathered together to share in a common purpose, to establish an intimate relationship with God and each other, and to reach the glorious destiny that God holds before us.

We have considered the biblical pictures of the church and seen what they teach about our corporate nature, our relationship with God, and our purpose. And we have recognised that the church should not be identified with 'the kingdom', 'national Israel' or 'the state'.

This has all helped us to establish an over-view of the church's life and ministry, and to appreciate that we are not meant to keep the Jewish law or duplicate the state's functions.

The more detailed teaching of the New Testament applies these principles and suggests that God's church has been 'gathered' to function in five main areas. These inter-relate, overlap and affect each other greatly, but all five functions need to be effectively fulfilled if the church is to be complete and balanced as God intends.

WORSHIP

The supreme, all-embracing call of the one church is to worship God. Before everything else, we are called to be a worshipping community.

What is worship?

The English word 'worship' means 'to attribute worth to something or someone'. It means 'worth-ship' – to give someone the honour or worth that they deserve.

Whenever we gather together, we should worship the Father, and acknowledge him for who he is – the Creator and Redeemer of the whole world. We should worship Jesus for who he is – the eternal Son and Saviour of all humanity. And we should worship the Holy Spirit – our enabler and encourager.

Christian worship is rooted in the Old Testament, especially in the Psalms: passages like Psalm 96:4, 8; 99:9 & 148:13 are as relevant today as when they were first written thousands of years ago.

There are two main Hebrew words for worship. *Hishahawah* literally means 'a bowing down', and suggests that worship is a bowing before God as a sign of respect. *Hishahawah* was the natural way for sinful

Psalm 96:4 ☐
96:8 ☐
99:9 ☐
148:13 ☐

people to approach their holy God – we see this, for example, in Psalm 95:6–11; 2 Kings 17:36 & 2 Chronicles 20:18.

The link between 'bowing down' or 'falling down' and 'worshipping the Lord' is repeated in the New Testament – for example, Matthew 2:11; 4:9; Acts 10:25; 1 Corinthians 14:24–25; Revelation 4:10; 5:14; 7:11–12; 11:16; 19:5, 10; 22:8.

The main Greek word for worship in the New Testament is *proskuneo*, which literally means 'to kiss towards'. We can think of this as 'making obeisance', 'revering' or 'paying homage': *proskuneo* suggests that all our worship should be inspired by adoring love.

When we meet together, but before we start to praise and thank God, we should spend time humbly recognising and remembering the greatness, holiness and immense love of our wonderful God.

The second main Hebrew word for worship is *abodah*, which means 'service'. This means that it is probably a tautology to speak about a worship service. True worship involves praising God with our mouths *and* serving him with our lives – we see this in Psalm 116:16–19.

A response

Worship is our response to God, which means that it is initiated by God. He inspired Israel to worship, he summoned them to worship, and he gave them precise instructions about the worship he sought.

In Exodus 10:26, Moses told Pharaoh that they would not know what worship to offer God until they reached the place where God was leading them. They knew that their worship had to be God-inspired and God-directed.

The worship described in Acts 2:11 and Romans 8:15–16 is a response to the work of the Spirit. When the Spirit truly comes upon us, our natural response should be to cry out in praise and worship to the Father. And Ephesians 5:18–20 shows that congregational worship is based in our experience of being filled with the Spirit.

John 4:23–24 states that the Father wants us to worship him 'in spirit and truth'. He is not much concerned with our musical tastes, but he aches for our hearts and minds to be right before him, for our lives to be always 'in the Spirit', and for our minds to be saturated in 'the truth'.

Psalm 95:6–11 ☐

2 Kings 17:36 ☐

2 Chronicles 20:18 ☐

Matthew 2:11 ☐
4:9 ☐

Acts 10:25 ☐

1 Corinthians 14:24–25 ☐

Revelation 4:10 ☐
5:14 ☐
7:11–12 ☐
11:16 ☐
19:5 ☐
19:10 ☐
22:8 ☐

Psalm 116:16–19 ☐

Exodus 10:26 ☐

Acts 2:11 ☐

Romans 8:15–16 ☐

Ephesians 5:18–20 ☐

John 4:23–24 ☐

Of course, we must make sure that our church worship is significant, meaningful, skilful and culturally relevant, for God does not want our worship to be dull, repetitive or boring. He wants us to worship him creatively, in fresh, exciting ways which reflect his own creative nature.

A sacrifice

We have seen in Part One that glory and sacrifice are bound together in the Scriptures. God's glory is revealed most clearly in self-sacrifice – which is why the cross, not the empty tomb or the dove – is the great symbol of the church.

Throughout the Bible, every aspect of human worship is linked with sacrifice: this is why God's glory is commonly experienced today in times of worship.

The principle of 2 Samuel 24:24 undergirds every scriptural idea about worship. In the Old Testament, people had to offer God the best that they had in sacrifice. Even though the era of bloody-sacrifices ended with Christ's once-and-for-all death on the cross, we are still called to offer sacrifices to God in the New Testament.

In particular, the church is called to worship God with:

- *the sacrifice of our bodies* – Romans 12:1; 15:16; Philippians 1:20; 2:17; 2 Timothy 4:6

- *the sacrifice of our money and possessions* – Hebrews 13:16; Matthew 6:24; 1 Timothy 6:10; Luke 6:38; 2 Corinthians 9:11–13

- *the sacrifice of our praises* – Hebrews 13:16; Psalm 66:1–4; Matthew 26:30; Acts 16:25; 1 Corinthians 14:26; Ephesians 5:19; Colossians 3:16; James 5:13

Biblical principles

The church's primary function is to worship God. If this is not central to every expression of the church, all the other activities will be out of line.

We examine worship much more fully in *Worship in spirit and truth* in this *Sword of the Spirit* series, but we should recognise three basic principles of church worship.

1. *Worship depends on the presence of the Holy Spirit*

   Philippians 3:3 states that we 'worship by the Spirit of God', and all our worship depends on him. Without him, we cannot speak to the Father. He inspires our praise and prayers, leads us into the truth, convicts us of sin, and gives us wonderful gifts to help us worship and serve God.

   Philippians 3:3 ☐

2. *Worship must be directed exclusively to God*

   The call of Psalm 34:3 is the eternal call to worship God. When the church's worship degenerates into performance or community hymn-singing it ceases to be worship.

   Psalm 34:3 ☐

3. *Worship must build up the body of Christ*

   Paul's great chapters about worship, 1 Corinthians 11–14, are dominated by the verb *oikodomeo*, which literally means 'to build a house', but is usually translated as the meaningless word 'edify'. 1 Corinthians 14:26 shows that every aspect of our worship should 'build together and build up' God's church.

   1 Corinthians 14:26 ☐

WORD

We saw in Part Two that the church is meant to be the 'keeper' or 'guardian' of eternal, absolute truth – the written word of God. Across the world today, there are many rival claims to truth; and, in Europe, we live in a post-modern culture which denies even the concept of absolute truth. This means that we need to teach and preach the truth with the greatest possible care and clarity.

It is of the utmost importance that we maintain our devotion to God's word. All sorts of emphases and fashions can distract us from scripture, but God's word must remain primary.

Every aspect of church life must be rooted in scripture. Every ministry must be based in biblical principles. Every believer needs constant encouragement to subordinate their thinking to God's word. New believers increasingly have no biblical background and a great mass of human ideas, so it is urgent that they are quickly taught the eternal principles of grace and faith.

Acts 2:11 ☐
        14–40 ☐

Acts 4:4 ☐

Acts 4:8–12 ☐
        8:4 ☐
        19:8–20 ☐

We see, in Acts 2:11, that the church began in worship but, in Acts 2:14–40, soon moved into the preaching of God's word. The Spirit fell, the disciples worshipped, but the people were only 'cut to the heart' when they heard the Word proclaimed in the power of the Spirit.

It is the same in Acts 3: a man was healed by the power of the Spirit, he praised God, but Acts 4:4 reports that it was the preaching of the Word which caused the people to believe.

The Bible shows that the early church took every opportunity to preach God's word – we see this in Acts 4:8–12; 8:4 & 19:8–20. And Acts 19:8–20 provides us with an outstanding example of Paul's devotion to the Word, and of the way God honoured his devotion.

Acts uses at least fifteen different Greek words to describe the great variety of ways that the early believers 'guarded' and used God's word. For example, they:

Acts 8:4 ☐

Acts 9:22 ☐

Acts 13:42 ☐

Acts 2:40 ☐

Acts 28:23 ☐

Acts 10:37 ☐

Acts 13:43 ☐

Acts 17:13 ☐

Acts 20:20 ☐

Acts 9:22 ☐

Acts 13:49 ☐

Acts 17:2 ☐

Acts 9:27–29 ☐

Acts 18:11 ☐

Acts 8:25 ☐

- *euangelizo*, 'announced' – Acts 8:4

- *suncheo*, 'confounded' – Acts 9:22

- *anangello*, 'declared' – Acts 20:20

- *parakaleo*, 'exhorted' – Acts 2:40

- *ektithemi*, 'explained' – Acts 28:23

- *kerusso*, 'heralded' – Acts 10:37

- *peitho*, 'persuaded' – Acts 13:43

- *katangello*, 'preached' – Acts 17:13

- *sumbibazo*, 'proved' – Acts 9:22

- *diaphero*, 'published' – Acts 13:49

- *dialegomai*, 'reasoned' – Acts 17:2

- *laleo*, 'spoke' – Acts 13:42

- *parrhesiazomai*, 'spoke boldly' – Acts 9:27–29

- *didasko*, 'taught' – Acts 18:11

- *diamarturomai*, 'testified' – Acts 8:25

Elsewhere in the New Testament, we read that the church also used God's word to argue, debate, expound, admonish, confess, charge, reprove, correct and instruct.

2 Timothy 3:15–17 alone should be enough to convince us of the vital importance of the Word in the life of the church. It reminds us that the Scriptures:

2 Timothy
3:15–17 ☐

- *make us wise for salvation*

- *are inspired by God*

- *are profitable for instruction in righteousness*

- *make us complete*

- *thoroughly equip us for every good work*

Throughout the New Testament, we are urged to 'keep' the Word and handle it carefully. Several principles emerge about the church and the Word. We must:

- *remember that it is God's word, God's oracles, God's mysteries* – 1 Peter 4:11; 1 Corinthians 4:1; 1 Thessalonians 2:13

1 Peter 4:11 ☐

1 Corinthians 4:1 ☐

1 Thessalonians
2:13 ☐

- *not hold to human traditions or be deceived by human ideas* – Mark 7:8–13; Colossians 2:8; 2 Peter 3:16

Mark 7:8–13 ☐

Colossians 2:8 ☐

2 Peter 3:16 ☐

- *guard it – but we can only do this by the Holy Spirit* – 2 Timothy 1:13–14

2 Timothy
1:13–14 ☐

- *handle it simply and directly, without twisting it* – the word for 'divide' in 2 Timothy 2:15, *orthotomounta*, is taken from road-making and means 'to cut straight'

2 Timothy 2:15 ☐

- *study it until we are thoroughly soaked in the Scriptures* – Colossians 3:16; Matthew 13:52

Colossians 3:16 ☐

Matthew 13:52 ☐

- *realise that it is incredibly powerful* – Isaiah 55:10–11; Jeremiah 23:29; Hebrews 4:12

Isaiah 55:10–11 ☐

Jeremiah 23:29 ☐

Hebrews 4:12 ☐

When any church moves away from the primary authority of God's word, as seen in the Scriptures, it starts to become incomplete, to be poorly equipped for good works, to be foolish in salvation.

If we neglect to 'keep' God's word central, we will not experience God's glory, and we will begin to wither and die.

WITNESS

We have repeatedly seen that the church has been called to reveal God's glory to all the nations. This means that the work of the church is witness.

John 15:26–27 ☐

Acts 1:8 ☐

John 15:26–27 & Acts 1:8 report the church's calling to be Jesus' witnesses – in words, deeds and lifestyle – to the ends of the earth. And the church has always exploded with growth whenever ordinary believers have been equipped and released as witnesses. Churches which do not burn with a passion for witness are missing the whole point of their calling – to go and make disciples of Jesus in all nations.

The Greek word *martureo*, 'to witness' means 'to speak about what has been seen or heard'. In the New Testament it is mainly used to describe the witness to Jesus by:

John 5:32 ☐
8:18 ☐

1 John 5:9–10 ☐

John 3:11 ☐
4:44 ☐
5:31 ☐
15:26 ☐

Hebrews 10:15 ☐

John 5:39 ☐

Hebrews 7:8 ☐
7:17 ☐

John 5:36 ☐
10:25 ☐

Acts 10:43 ☐
23:11 ☐

1 Corinthians
15:15 ☐

John 1:27 ☐
3:28–30 ☐
15:18 ☐

- *the Father* – John 5:32; 8:18; 1 John 5:9–10

- *Jesus himself* – John 3:11; 4:44; 5:31

- *the Holy Spirit* – John 15:26; Hebrews 10:15

- *the Scriptures* – John 5:39; Hebrews 7:8, 17

- *the works of Jesus* – John 5:36; 10:25

- *prophets and apostles* – Acts 10:43; 23:11; 1 Corinthians 15:15

This emphasises that all our words and activities are meant to point people to him: we are witnesses to Jesus, not to ourselves or to our expression of the church.

John's words in John 1:27 and 3:28–30 are very relevant today. Our goal must be to testify to Jesus, to attract people to him, to encourage them to follow him, to assist them to love him, and so on.

We must always remember that we cannot witness effectively to Jesus in our own strength and ability. We need the help of the Spirit. John 15:18 reminds us that he is 'The Witness', and we can only become witnesses as we allow him to work in our lives.

In Acts 1:8, the disciples were told that they had to wait for the power of the Spirit to come upon them before they could be witnesses, and this is still true for the church today.

Witnessing is not a specialised activity which the church occasionally carries out – it encapsulates everything that we say and do. The truth is that we are all always witnessing to Jesus; sadly, much of what we say and do neither brings him much glory nor attracts many people to him.

We examine witnessing in some detail in *Reaching the Lost* in this *Sword of the Spirit* series, but we should recognise that it includes:

- *preaching*

- *social concern*

- *personal evangelism*

- *dialogue and debate*

- *healing*

- *deliverance*

- *celebration*

- *signs and wonders*

- *literature*

- *the arts*

The church desperately needs the guidance of the Spirit to find appropriate ways of witnessing which will reach our generation and culture. But, ultimately, the most effective witnesses are always believers who live the ordinary dedicated life of Jesus, and gossip the good news in language that the people around them understand.

WELFARE

Some churches are so evangelistic that they ignore pastoral care, and others do the reverse. We must find a godly balance and ensure that the people in our churches are properly pastored.

In John 21:15–17, Peter was first commissioned to 'feed my lambs', then to 'tend my sheep', and finally to 'feed my sheep'. Verses 15 and 17 use the Greek verb *bosko*, which means 'to nourish', whereas verse 16 uses *poimaino*, which means 'to tend' or 'to act as a shepherd'.

John 21:15–17 ☐

This shows that the feeding of God's flock from the word of God is a constant and regular requirement: it is the priority. Tending the flock – acting as one of Christ's under-shepherds – involves discipline, authority, restoration and practical help, but these are incidental in comparison with the feeding.

This does not mean that the welfare of the church should be restricted to visiting when someone is ill or bereaved. Instead, welfare means the sort of practical caring described in John 13:2–14; Acts 4:34–37; 6:1–7 & 11:27–30; and it means obeying Jesus' John 13:31–35 commandment.

John 13:2–14 □

Acts 4:34–37 □
    6:1–7 □
    11:27–30 □

John 13:31–35 □

John 13:31–35 weaves together revealing glory, witnessing effectively and practical welfare. As we have noted, the church's five functions overlap and inter-relate, but they all need to be effectively fulfilled if the church is to be complete and balanced as God intends.

Acts 2:40–47 □
    4:31–37 □

Acts 2:40–47 and 4:31–37 suggest that the practical caring of the early church was an important factor in its dynamic attractiveness. In fact, it is almost impossible to disentangle 'worship', 'welfare', 'word' and 'witness' in these passages; they are both magnificent examples of a church which is functioning effectively in the Spirit – bringing glory to God and reaching out to the people around.

Of course, we are also called to care for the welfare of the community around us as well. No church should neglect community care as Jesus calls us to serve *with* him, but we must take care not to duplicate or usurp the state's distinctive functions.

Community care must become an even greater church emphasis when society disintegrates, social needs grow, and governments abdicate from their responsibilities to the elderly, the homeless, the mentally ill, and other socially disadvantaged groups.

It is worth remembering that God has commonly sent revival to churches which were deeply involved in controversial community care programmes. For example, in the 1860s, the North American churches that experienced revival were principally those which were resisting slavery and caring practically for escaped and ex-slaves.

And, a few years later, the British 'evangelical awakening' occurred essentially among the churches which were deeply concerned with industrial, educational, penal and mental health reform, and were caring practically for abused, destitute and illiterate children.

WARFARE

We have noticed that Matthew 16:18 implies the church will be involved with warfare. We know that the people of God in the Old Testament had to fight every inch of the way to possess the promised land. We have learnt that every Greek city assembly had an important military function. And we have seen that the church is called to reveal God's glory not just to the nations of earth but also to all the principalities and powers in the heavenly places.

Matthew 16:18 ☐

This means we must realise that the church is not able to do the work of Jesus without grappling with the spiritual forces which are opposed to God's kingdom. We examine warfare in Part Seven of *Effective Prayer* and see that it involves the whole of the church's life.

Ephesians 6:10–18 describes the church at war and offers a picture of God's army standing shoulder-to-shoulder and fighting in hand-to-hand combat. The whole point of the passage is prayer. We wear God's armour so that we can be ready to engage the enemy when we pray.

Ephesians 6:10–18 ☐

Three important Old Testament passages teach us some important principles about warfare.

Daniel 10:12–21 shows that:

Daniel 10:12–21 ☐

- *demonic beings exist and try to oppose God's work*
- *they are associated with temporal and territorial areas*
- *there is a link between heavenly and earthly activity*
- *Daniel achieved a spiritual breakthrough by his prayers*

Exodus 17:8–16 teaches that spiritual victory depends on:

Exodus 17:8–16 ☐

- *following God's directions*
- *the right use of God's authority*
- *God's people working together in unity*
- *persistent prayer*

And 1 Chronicles 14:8–17 suggests that we must:

1 Chronicles 14:8–17 ☐

- *be in our stronghold, in the Lord*
- *be led and guided by the Lord*

- *work in partnership with the Lord*

- *expect the enemy to persist in their attacks*

- *wait for God to act on our behalf*

Ephesians 6:10–18 shows that we should equip ourselves for warfare with God's personal Isaiah 59:15–19 armour. This represents truths about our lifestyle, and the Greek word used means that we put it on only once – though we must walk in it every day.

The church does need to confront demonic powers through prayer, fasting and praise, but we need to do it cautiously, under the direction of the Spirit – not rashly, five times in every meeting! Warfare prayer is on God's agenda, but we must be clearly directed by the Spirit in everything we do.

But warfare involves even more than this. Luke 10:19 suggests that we have been given Christ's authority to trample over all the power of the enemy, and this involves matters like:

- *warning about the dangers of the occult*

- *casting out demons*

- *releasing those who are oppressed by the devil*

- *establishing God's rule in society by acting as 'salt' and 'light'*

- *resisting temptation*

- *preaching the gospel*

- *speaking God's prophetic words*

- *rejecting mammon*

The church has a vicious enemy, and 1 Peter 5:8–9 reminds us both that he is seeking people to devour, and also that we can resist him – if we are steadfast in the faith. Jesus' Matthew 16:18 promise is absolute, but it is meaningless unless the church is actively raiding the enemy's kingdom, resisting his forces and releasing his captives.

Isaiah 59:15–19 ☐

Luke 10:19 ☐

1 Peter 5:8–9 ☐

Matthew 16:18 ☐

PART TEN

the sacraments of the church

The English word 'sacrament' is derived from the Latin word *sacramentum*, which literally means 'a solemn oath'. *Sacramentum* was used in early Christian literature to translate the Greek word *musterion* which is often used in the New Testament – for example, in Matthew 13:11; Mark 4:11; Luke 8:10; Romans 16:25; 1 Corinthians 4:1; Ephesians 3:9; Colossians 1:27; 1 Timothy 3:9; Revelation 10:7.

Musterion has always been translated into English as 'mystery', but 'sacrament' has been absorbed into English as a technical word for a 'sign of God's grace'.

Today, we use the word 'sacrament' to identify an act which is regarded as 'an outward and visible sign of inward and spiritual grace'.

The medieval church identified seven acts as sacraments: baptism, confirmation, the Lord's Supper, penance, anointing the dying with oil, ordination and marriage. Eastern Orthodox Churches and Roman Catholics still believe that these acts are sacraments, but Protestant churches maintain that Christ ordained or instituted only two: baptism and the Lord's Supper.

Matthew 13:11 ☐

Mark 4:11 ☐

Luke 8:10 ☐

Romans 16:25 ☐

1 Corinthians 4:1 ☐

Ephesians 3:9 ☐

Colossians 1:27 ☐

1 Timothy 3:9 ☐

Revelation 10:7 ☐

Baptism and the Lord's Supper are 'sacraments' or 'mysteries' because they are 'outward, visible signs' of the blessing of the gospel; They have been given to the church by God's grace as powerful demonstrations of his life in the body. We receive them by faith, and they are central to the life of most churches. In fact, there can be no real expression of a biblical church without them.

Signs of grace

It is critical we understand that baptism and the Lord's Supper – 'communion' – are signs of God's grace and not merely signs of human activity. Primarily, they are signs of God's good will towards us. Only secondarily, in the realm of faith, are they signs of our belief.

If baptism and communion were simply actions which expressed belief, they would not be 'mysteries' and, therefore, they would not be 'sacraments'.

The fact that they are 'mysteries' is evidenced by our own experience. Although we may struggle to explain what exactly happens in communion and baptism, we instinctively recognise that God is in them in a special way. Time and again we 'feel' that God is powerfully present at the church services of communion and baptism.

The 'mysterious' nature of the sacraments is also evidenced by the controversy and division in the church about them – both down the centuries, and across and within the traditions today.

Sadly, many Spirit-filled leaders who are united in their commitment to the gospel, who minister in the gifts of the Spirit, who have fruitful, anointed ministries, are still divided by their views on baptism and communion.

Focused on the cross

Even though church leaders often have different views about baptism and communion, they are united in recognising their importance. This is because both sacraments have clearly been instituted by Christ.

Jesus told his followers to 'make disciples of all nations, baptising them in the name of the Father and of the Son and of the Holy Spirit'; and to 'do this in remembrance of me' – Matthew 28:19 & Luke 22:19.

Matthew 28:19 ☐

Luke 22:19 ☐

However, both sacraments are also important because they point directly to the sacrifice of Jesus – to the cross, the most potent sign of grace. In many ways, baptism is a re-enactment of Christ's death and resurrection in which the believer shares by faith; and communion is a dramatic reminder that we all have to go on sharing in his broken body and shed blood by faith.

We have seen that God reveals his glory most clearly in sacrifice and at the place of self-sacrifice, so it is little wonder that we 'feel' his 'glorious' presence most strongly at times of baptism and communion.

Gifts to the church

It is also important that we do not fall into the trap of regarding the sacraments as institutions *of* the church, as activities which go on *within* the church. Baptism and communion were instituted by Christ *for* his church – they are two special gifts *to* the church.

We will understand them more easily when we realise that the church itself is the ultimate 'sacrament', for the body of Christ is surely the most obvious 'outward and visible sign of inward and spiritual grace'.

For example, we know that the church is a 'mystery' for none of us fully grasps the truths of passages like Ephesians 2:14–15. And we should be able to grasp that the church is 'the' sacrament of Christ's presence and action and grace in the world.

Ephesians
2:14–15 ☐

We also appreciate the sacraments better when we think about them as 'instruments of grace'. Whether we consider salvation, Christian ministries, or the gifts of the Spirit, the basic principle is always the same: the initiative is God's, his freely-given gifts express his grace; we have to receive them with faith.

God does not work independently of our will, he does not force salvation, or tongues, or service, upon us. Equally, we can not create them ourselves or 'make' anything happen: we cannot save ourselves, heal anyone or interpret a tongue. Instead, we receive them as gifts from God by faith.

God takes every possible opportunity to underline the fact that he wants a relationship with us – a partnership in and with the Spirit. Our hand of faith is meant to grasp his hand of grace, and we are meant to walk with him, being led by him at all times.

It is much the same with baptism and communion. They are gifts from God which have distinctive purposes, but they have to be 'unwrapped' and received by faith. For example, we know that the gifts of the Spirit have been given to 'edify' the church – to build us up and build us together so that we can serve God more effectively.

We do not need to understand 'how' the gifts build the church; we simply need to know that they do, and that – without our faith – they cannot. We begin to understand baptism and communion more fully when we start to think about them in a similar way.

BAPTISM

The Greek verb *baptizo*, 'to baptise' is a form of *bapto*, 'to dip' and can mean to 'plunge', 'sink', 'drown', 'drench', 'overwhelm', 'immerse' or 'saturate'. As we have a 'religious' understanding of baptism today, it is important we realise that it was an ordinary, everyday word in New Testament times.

In New Testament times, *baptizo* was used in two ways. It was the common word for:

- *dyeing a garment by 'dipping' it in a container of dye*

- *collecting liquid by 'dipping' a cup or jug into a bowl or barrel*

The first use suggests that Christian baptism will involve being plunged into something which accomplishes a change as complete as dyeing. We can expect to take on something of the colour and character of whatever it is that we are dipped into.

The second use suggests that, in baptism, we are meant to be filled with whatever we are dipped into.

Jewish background

Baptizo has an important Jewish background which helps us to understand what to expect in baptism. *Tabal*, the equivalent Hebrew word, is used in the Old Testament to describe:

- *the priestly act of dipping in sacrificial blood as part of the Passover and the sin offering* – Exodus 12:22; Leviticus 4:6, 17

- *priestly dipping in oil to cleanse lepers and allow them back into society* – Leviticus 14:16

- *priestly dipping in blood for purification* – Leviticus 14:6, 51

- *the dipping of Joseph's coat in blood* – Genesis 37:31

- *the dipping of Naaman in the Jordan for healing* – 2 Kings 5:14

Exodus 12:22 ☐

Leviticus 4:6 ☐

4:17 ☐

14:16 ☐

14:6 ☐

14:51 ☐

Genesis 37:31 ☐

2 Kings 5:14 ☐

This background means that we can expect Christian baptism to have something to do with being dipped in sacrificial, Passover blood for cleansing from sin, and with being dipped in oil for healing and incorporation into the people of God.

Although it is not recorded in the Scriptures, we know that Gentiles who wanted to convert to Judaism had to baptise themselves – to dip themselves in water like Naaman – in the presence of witnesses. First, the men were circumcised; then the men, women and children all baptised themselves to wash away their Gentile impurities; finally, they presented the sacrificial offering. They were then regarded as Israelites.

This part of the Jewish background suggests that we may expect Christian baptism to have a place in the process of conversion – to be one aspect of becoming a member of the family of God.

New Testament baptism

Baptism in the New Testament differed from its Jewish foreshadowing in two important ways:

- *nobody baptised themselves* – it was always something done by another, as baptism is essentially a sign of what God has done for us

- *the noun* baptisma, *'baptism' suddenly appeared* – it had not been used before in the Greek language, which suggests that Christian baptism is something new

John's 'baptism of repentance' is the first mention of baptism in the New Testament – Luke 3:3. It was a baptism 'for, *eis* (with a view to), the forgiveness of sins.

Luke 3:3 ☐

John did not claim that his baptism forgave sins, instead his baptism helped people to repent and turn away from sins: we can say that it was a repentance-baptism. In contrast, Christian baptism is essentially a belief-baptism.

Although Jesus did not need to repent and turn from sin, he fulfilled Isaiah 53:12 by identifying with the sinners who were being baptised. At his baptism, Mark 1:10 reports that the Spirit came down upon him, and from then on Jesus is described as being full of the Spirit.

John 3:22 & John 4:1–2 show that baptism was associated with becoming one of Jesus' disciples, and Matthew 28:19 reports that we have been commanded to baptise believers as part of making them disciples.

In the New Testament, baptism is said to include the following elements:

- *forgiveness of sin* – Acts 2:38

- *cleansing from sins* – Acts 22:16; 1 Corinthians 6:11

- *union with Christ* – Galatians 3:27

- *union with Christ in his death and resurrection* – Romans 6:3–4; Colossians 2:11–12

- *participation in Christ's sonship* – Galatians 3:26–27

- *consecration to God* – 1 Corinthians 6:11

- *membership in the body of Christ* – Acts 2:41–47 Galatians 3:27–29

- *possession of the Spirit* – Acts 2:38; 1 Corinthians 6:11; 12:13

- *new life in the Spirit* – Titus 3:5–6; John 3:5

- *grace to live God's life according to his will* – Romans 6:1–14; Colossians 2:12–3:17

- *the inheritance of the kingdom of God* – John 3:5

This list of the elements of baptism is an all-embracing description of God's saving grace, and many people struggle to understand what an outward act like baptism can have to do with these inner spiritual transformations.

Throughout the ages, church leaders have usually taken one of three different and opposed approaches:

Isaiah 53:12 ☐

Mark 1:10 ☐

John 3:22 ☐
    4:1–2 ☐

Matthew 28:19 ☐

Acts 2:38 ☐
    22:16 ☐

1 Corinthians
    6:11 ☐

Galatians
    3:26–27 ☐

Romans 6:3–4 ☐

Colossians
    2:11–12 ☐

1 Corinthians
    6:11 ☐

Acts 2:41–47 ☐

Galatians
    3:27–29 ☐

Acts 2:38 ☐

Titus 3:5–6 ☐

John 3:5 ☐

Romans 6:1–14 ☐

Colossians
    2:12–3:17 ☐

1. *The sign of baptism always conveys the gift.* When someone is baptised, all the promised elements are automatically applied in their life.

    But Jesus warned us, in Matthew 7:21–23, about the dangers of doing the right things and not knowing him personally; Romans 2:29 shows that external signs need to be evidenced by spiritual realities; and justification is always by grace through faith and never through baptism. We see this particularly clearly in 1 Peter 3:18–22.

    Matthew 7:21–23 ☐
    Romans 2:29 ☐

    1 Peter 3:18–22 ☐

2. *The sign achieves nothing at all.* It is simply a symbol of human belief. Nothing happens spiritually when someone is baptised. It is merely a human 'amen' to what God has already done and an act of witness to other people.

    But this idea has more to do with a historic reaction to the first view and with human intellectual difficulties at the idea of a sacrament. It is very difficult to justify this view from the New Testament – which never actually describes baptism as an act of witness. We simply must accept that the New Testament really does closely link baptism with the blessing of the gospel.

    At a very simple level, we can see that a kiss is not only a sign of love, it also increases the love; and a hug is not only a sign of friendship it also enhances the relationship. This is also true of baptism and communion.

3. *The sign seals, pledges or confirms the gift.* It is a *sacramentum*, a divine 'solemn oath'. Thought about this way, baptism is rather like the title deed to property. Certain conditions still need to be fulfilled, the new owner must still personally 'experience' or possess the property – it is not enough merely to possess the tile deed. Yet we cannot pretend that the title deed is an unimportant document.

    We know that faith, in the Bible, means believing a promise of God, claiming it for ourselves, and then believing the truth of it even before the promise is worked out in our experience.

    When we think about it this way, baptism is the 'solemn oath' or pledge of the salvation promises of God. As soon as someone has been baptised in faith, they can look forward with faith to the fulfilment of these promises in their experience.

Baptism and grace

Hebrews 10:22 ☐

Every passage about baptism, except Hebrews 10:22, stresses that it is the name of Christ, the resurrection of Christ, the Holy Spirit, or the Word of God or Christ which brings about the elements of baptism. And even Hebrews 10 relates baptism to the work of Christ.

Romans 6 ☐

Colossians 2:12 ☐

This means that God himself is at work in the believers who are being baptised. Romans 6 and Colossians 2:12 use the passive form to underline the gracious action of God in baptism. These passages suggest that, just as God worked in Jesus in the resurrection, so he works in a similar way in believers who are baptised. This means that baptism is an occasion when God deals graciously with us.

Baptism and faith

We can think of baptism as the embodiment of the gospel, as a representation of redemption. Christ's redeeming death has made new life possible for all people, and we 'participate' – *koinonia* – in his new life by 'participating' in him. This presupposes some act of human will.

Throughout the New Testament, the same gifts of grace are associated with both baptism and faith, and it is always assumed that faith leads to baptism and that baptism is for faith. We can say that, in the New Testament, baptism is the 'divinely appointed rendezvous of grace for faith'. It is 'the crowning moment of the act of faith'.

Put simply, we need faith:

- *before baptism* – so that Christ and his gospel may be confessed in baptism

- *in baptism* – to receive God's gracious gifts and promises

- *after baptism* – to 'abide' in the grace he has given, to work out the grace he has worked within us, to experience all the promised elements of faith and baptism

Baptism and the Spirit

It is clear that, in the New Testament, the anointing with the Spirit usually takes place alongside baptism. But the Spirit is received by grace through faith, not automatically in and through baptism.

It is also clear that we cannot really separate the Spirit from Christ and his gifts of grace – for the Spirit is Christ's ultimate grace gift to the church. Where Christ is, there is his Spirit. We are either in Christ or we are not in Christ, and either we have the Spirit or we do not – as Romans 8:9 makes clear.

Romans 8:9 ☐

This means that baptism in the name of Christ, which is a 'putting on' of Christ, cannot be divorced from baptism in the Spirit and a 'putting on' of the Spirit.

True baptism, in an authentic New Testament context, is always linked to a baptism of the Spirit – a dipping in holy oil and a filling with living water.

Baptism and the church

If baptism is into Christ it must also be a baptism into the church. It cannot be anything else for the church is the body of Christ. We see this in 1 Corinthians 12:13.

1 Corinthians 12:13 ☐

This idea seems to be basic to Paul's understanding, for in many passages he leaps straight from writing about baptism to teaching about the church – for example, Galatians 3:27–28.

Galatians 3:27–28 ☐

This means that baptism has both a personal and a corporate aspect: it involves us personally with Christ and corporately with his body.

In Acts 2:40, each individual convert separated themselves by their baptism from the unbelievers around them and numbered themselves among the followers of Jesus. This is one reason why baptism should be a visible, public action.

Acts 2:40 ☐

We must try to recover the significance of baptism for the church and re-establish its centrality. In the New Testament, the outward act of baptism witnessed to a believer's outward entry into the church in that locality, but it also coincided with baptism in the Spirit and incorporation into the one body of Christ.

Somehow we must work at finding ways to express and under-line this truth today. We must also constantly stress the place of our faith in baptism whilst never overlooking the wonder of God's grace.

THE LORD'S SUPPER

As we saw earlier, the Lord's Supper is the *koinonia*, the 'communion' or 'fellowship meal', and a central feature of church life.

The bread and wine of communion represent the continuing life of Christ in the Christian community; and we can think of baptism as 'the sacrament of Christian initiation' and of communion as 'the sacrament of Christian participation'. We are not only baptised into new life, we must also continue to participate in that life: communion is a gift from God which gives us that opportunity.

As a sacrament, communion is no mere memorial service; it is a living encounter with the risen Lord. All that Christ has done for us at the cross, and all that we have received from him by faith, is powerfully confirmed and continually sealed as we faithfully participate in communion.

Unlike baptism, the fellowship meal does not bring us into anything new; rather, it renews in us what we already have. And whereas baptism is to be administered once, pledging and confirming our entrance into Christ, communion is to be shared regularly and repeatedly, confirming and sealing our on-going fellowship with Christ and each other.

Mark 14:17–26 ☐

Luke 22:14–20 ☐

Acts 2:42–46 ☐

20:7 ☐

1 Corinthians
11:17–34 ☐

The Lord's Supper is based on the last meal that Jesus ate with his apostles, in Mark 14:17–26 & Luke 22:14–20, before the cross; and it soon became the centre-point of fellowship and worship in the early church, where it was called 'the breaking of bread' – we see this in Acts 2:42–46; 20:7 and 1 Corinthians 11:17–34.

Jewish background

Matthew
26:17–30 ☐

Mark 14:12–26 ☐

Luke 22:7–38 ☐

John 13:1 ☐

Jesus' last meal was part of the Passover festival. It is not clear whether it was the main Passover meal itself, as Matthew 26:17–30; Mark 14:12–26; Luke 22:7–38 suggest, or a festive meal just before the Passover, as John 13:1 suggests.

Either way, the meal was clearly rooted in the Passover, and it is not possible to appreciate the Lord's Supper fully without some awareness of the Passover meal which lies behind it.

The Passover meal was rooted in the deliverance of Israel from Egypt which is recorded in Exodus 11:1–13:16. In Jesus' day, the meal involved four principle aspects.

Exodus
11:1–13:16 ☐

1. *The people looked back* – they remembered God's mercy in delivering them from slavery in Egypt.

   They did this by re-telling the story of the Exodus as if nobody had heard it before, and by re-living their deliverance. They ate both bitter herbs to share in 'the bitterness of slavery' and unleavened bread which they called 'the bread of affliction which our Fathers ate when they came out of Egypt'.

2. *The people looked in* – they purified themselves and their homes from anything which was evil or dirty.

   Before the feats, there was a time of personal purification and domestic 'spring-cleaning'. Before the Passover could be held, every trace of corruption had to be removed.

3. *The people looked around* – the feast was not a private affair, it was thoroughly corporate.

   The whole family took part in the meal. The eldest woman was honoured, one guest was singled out for a special privilege, the children were asked questions – and even had a small game of 'hide-and-seek' as they searched for the bread that had been hidden.

4. *The people looked forward* – they looked forward to the Messiah and his new age and prayed for his coming.

   They laid an extra place, with an empty chair opposite, for the Elijah who would prepare the way for the Messiah. The front door was left ajar for him, and the children were sent out to see if he was coming. The family looked forward to salvation by saying, 'This year we are here; next year in the land of Israel. This year we are slaves; next year free men!'

It is obvious that the church's fellowship meal has been greatly shaped by the Passover. All these four elements are present in Communion – and, it is worth noting, they can also be seen in baptism.

Communion looks back

Luke 22:19 ☐

1 Corinthians
11:23–35 ☐

In Luke 22:19, Jesus told us to 'do this in remembrance of me'. We are called to remember with thanksgiving God's grace and mercy in delivering us from the slavery of sin through the once-and-for-all death of Jesus – the true Paschal lamb. We see this at work in 1 Corinthians 11:23–35.

Just as the Passover meal was a continuing memorial of God's saving work in the Exodus, and as the rainbow is a continuing sign of God's saving work in the Flood, so communion is both a sign and an abiding memorial of God's saving work on the cross.

But that is not all, for we also re-live our personal application of the cross. The bread and the wine are not empty signs, they are God's 'solemn oath' – the pledge or confirmation of God's mercy and forgiveness.

The Old Testament contains a wealth of teaching on the place and value of memorials. There were memorial objects, memorial offerings, memorial feasts and memorial days. These were given to help the people of Israel to remember some mighty act of God or to accompany some great promise of God.

Exodus 12:14 ☐

Esther 9:28 ☐

These memorials were intended to keep Israel's faith alive, and to keep her in touch with the God of history. They were often given as a special provision for children – so that the experience of God could be passed on to the next generation, and they would know the God of Israel and participate in his goodness. We see this, for example, in Exodus 12:14 and Esther 9:28.

In a similar way, when we take part in communion, we remember the presence and power of Christ among his people, we celebrate his victory over sin and death, and we claim our part in that activity.

Genesis 9:16–17 ☐

Exodus 2:24–25 ☐

Memorials are also equally important reminders to God. We see this in Genesis 9:16–17 & Exodus 2:24–25. This means that when we take communion, God is present to fulfil every promise signified by the memorial. Because communion is a memorial, whatever the bread and wine symbolises is available by faith to all who receive it.

At communion, we do not just remember Christ's sacrifice on the cross, we claim it for ourselves, we 'fellowship' or share in it. Our physical receiving of the bread and wine emphasises this important truth.

Communion looks in

1 Corinthians 11:17–34 underlines the importance of preparing ourselves before communion. Before receiving the bread and the wine, we should examine ourselves, confess what we know to be wrong, and ask God to forgive and cleanse us.

1 Corinthians
11:17–34 ☐

We come to communion recognising that it is sign of God's grace, and so we come trusting in Christ's righteousness and not in our own worthiness. We come in humble repentance, seeking mercy and forgiveness for our wrong thoughts and actions.

This self-examination is not to prevent us from taking part; rather it is to bring us to the meal ready to meet the Lord with clean hands and a pure heart – we can think of it as like washing hands before eating.

The nature of communion means that we are encouraged to come with our needs. If the communion is a memorial and participation in the benefits of the cross, we can come expecting our needs to be met. We should expect to be strengthened and nourished in our faith, renewed in our spiritual experience and healed in our body.

Communion looks around

Communion is not a private matter, it is 'the' expression of the church's *koinonia*. All God's family – the men, women and children of the 'household', and any guests and visitors – assemble together to celebrate their communion with each other and God.

We know that the church is a family, and this is the family meal. We have seen that communion is built upon the Passover – which was celebrated by families in their homes – and that it is related to the Old Testament memorials which were instituted, in part, to pass on the experience of God to new generations.

It is tragic, therefore, that some churches have formalised the fellowship meal into some sort of ritual, that others have lost the sense of festive joy which characterised the Passover, and that many have removed the sense of community: several churches celebrate communion only when children are absent, and some even refuse to allow visitors to participate.

Communion is a meal of covenant and fellowship which is meant to strengthen the body. Eating together, fellowshipping together in the body and blood of Christ, is a very important part of being *koinonia* and *ekklesia*.

Communion looks forward

1 Corinthians
11:26 ☐

1 Corinthians 11:26 states that communion is 'until he comes'. In communion, we look forward, full of hope, to the coming of the Bridegroom, to the 'marriage feast of the lamb'.

Unlike the Jews, we believe that the Messiah has come, and that his reign has begun. But we know that his kingdom has not yet come in all its fullness, that we are 'living in the overlap'. We examine this idea in *The Rule of God*. This means that, like the Jews, we should live 'with the door open', always alert and attentive for the return of our lover.

The 'real presence'

Just as many Christian leaders disagree about what happens in baptism, so they also offer a variety of views on the mystery of communion. There are four main explanations as to how we experience the presence of Christ in communion.

1. The traditional Catholic view is that Christ is present in the Communion through the process of 'transubstantiation'. The *substance* of the bread and wine are said to change, actually and physically, into the very *substance* of the body and blood of Jesus.

    This is based in the belief that Jesus was speaking literally rather than metaphorically when he said 'This is my body'.

2. Martin Luther believed that the body and blood of Christ were present in the bread and wine, but not in the way that Catholics taught. He rejected their view that the bread and wine were replaced by the substance of Christ's body and blood. Instead, he maintained that the body and blood are contained 'in, with and under the bread and wine'. This is known as 'consubstantiation'. This still means that we take the body and blood of Jesus whenever we eat the bread and wine.

3. Huldrych Zwingli, a sixteenth century Swiss theologian and contemporary of Luther, rejected the Catholic and Lutheran views.

He taught that the bread and wine were purely symbolic. It was his view that Christ was present by the Spirit at all times, and that communion does not significantly add to our experience of Christ's presence – other than the obvious benefits which flow from remembering him.

These three views still predominate in different branches of the church, with most evangelicals and pentecostals following Zwingli. A fourth view, however, is closer to the biblical teaching.

4. John Calvin, another sixteenth century Swiss theologian, was the great architect of Reformation Theology. He taught what has come to be known as 'receptionism'. Like Zwingli, he believed that Christ is present by the Spirit when we take Communion, and that the bread and wine remain unchanged. But Calvin insisted that – when the bread and wine are received by someone whose faith is genuine and active – something spiritual is received from God.

   Calvin's view is that sacraments are signs and seals of God's covenant, and that in communion (and baptism) God seals the grace that the sacraments signify.

This means that to take communion, in the full New Testament sense, in faith, is to experience a powerful operation of the Holy Spirit who manifests the real presence of Christ in a special way which strengthens and enriches our spiritual lives. As such, we can see that communion is a vital part of a healthy church's life.

Spiritual food

At communion, the Anglican liturgy encourages believers to 'Feed on him in your hearts by faith with thanksgiving'. This helpful phrase stresses that communion is food for our spiritual life. In some mysterious way that we do not fully understand, Christ communicates his life to us as we receive the bread and wine. And so we fellowship with him, feeding on him by faith.

The imagery of flesh and blood occurs throughout John 6, and this seems to be point towards communion and to the 'Word of God' as the fulfilment of the 'Wisdom of God' in Proverbs 8:1–9:12 who cries, 'Come, eat of my bread and drink of the wine I have mixed. Forsake foolishness and live.'

John 6 ☐

Proverbs
8:1–9:12 ☐

John 6:47–57 ☐

1 Corinthians 10 ☐

In John 6, especially in verses 47–57, Jesus shows how central communion is to the Christian life. It is a feeding and fellowshipping in his body and blood; and, by it, Jesus confirms to us his life, his indwelling presence and his provision of spiritual nourishment. This is confirmed by 1 Corinthians 10 where Paul compares communion with the spiritual food and drink that Israel was given in the wilderness.

Covenant meal

Matthew 26:28 ☐

Mark 14:24 ☐

1 Corinthians
    11:25 ☐

Matthew 26:28; Mark 14:24 and 1 Corinthians 11:25 state that the wine represents the blood of the new covenant. In the Scriptures, God's relationship with his people is often expressed in the form of blood covenants, whereby the blood indicates the binding nature of the covenant: blood is both the pledge and the sign of the covenant. We consider this in Part Nine of *Living Faith*.

The New Covenant supersedes the Old Covenant, and communion is the meal at which we renew our participation in the covenant: we renew our commitment to covenant obedience and pledge again our loyalty to the Lord.

But it is also the occasion when the Lord seals in our hearts the benefits of the covenant and works in our lives to fulfil the covenant promises. We can say that the covenant promises are not just exhibited in communion, they are also executed through communion; and that they are not just modelled in communion, they are also manifested through communion.

As we take the bread and wine we take hold of the covenant promises, we thank God for them, and we enter into everything that the blood has purchased for us.

Spiritual oneness

Communion also enhances our oneness in Christ. As we share communion, we are drawn together as members of our local fellowship, and we also experience our union with all God's people in the universal church.

We can say that, by participating in communion, we both demonstrate and develop our oneness in Christ: communion is much, much more than a visual aid or symbolic act of unity.

1 Corinthians 10:17 states that we are one body *because* we share in one bread, and sharing in the church's fellowship meal is one of the most effective ways we have of developing our cross-forged oneness. This means that communion is as much about fellowship with each other as it is fellowship with God.

1 Corinthians 11 stresses the importance of repairing relationships among believers as part of our preparation for communion. When we take communion we should consider each other, put away anything which hinders fellowship, and ensure that broken relationships are mended in a godly spirit of forgiveness and reconciliation.

Thanksgiving

Some sections of the church call the Lord's Supper, 'The Eucharist'. This comes from the Greek word *eucharisteo*, which means 'to thank', and refers to Jesus' prayer of thanksgiving or blessing over the bread and wine at the last supper. We see this in Matthew 26:26–27; Mark 14:22–23 & 1 Corinthians 11:23–24.

Too many communion services are morbid memorials riddled by dry ritual rather than glorious celebrations throbbing with thanksgiving.

When we begin to grasp the true sacramental nature of communion – when we realise all that God pledges and confirms in communion, and appreciate all that we can receive by faith at communion – it naturally becomes an occasion for great thanksgiving in the church.

Central

We must never overlook the significance of Paul's teaching in 1 Corinthians 11–14. In these chapters, he weaves together worship, communion, the gifts of the Spirit and the primacy of love. This suggests that those churches which stress the gifts should also make much of communion, and that the gifts should be an important part of communion.

We have seen that the 'breaking of bread', the Lord's Supper, is central in the life of the New Testament church: it is 'the' expression of *koinonia* – of sharing together with Christ and with each other, and so should be more central in our church life today.

1 Corinthians 10:17 ☐

1 Corinthians 11 ☐

Matthew 26:26–27 ☐

Mark 14:22–23 ☐

1 Corinthians 11:23–24 ☐

In the communion meal, we gather together to be with each other and the Lord: we remember, we give thanks, we love, we look to the future with confidence, we receive from God, we are strengthened for service, and we are built up and built together as the body.

PART ELEVEN

the spirit and the church

It is easy to study the Bible with the help of a book like this, and just to make a list of the changes that we need to make in 'our' church.

We could conclude that 'our' expression of the church would function more effectively if only we had a balanced involvement with worship, word, witness, welfare and warfare; or if we had a more biblical structure and style of leadership; or if we stressed the corporate dimension of church life and made baptism and communion more central.

All these are important, but quite useless on their own. If we are to function effectively, and reveal God's glory in the world, we must be closer to the Holy Spirit. The church needs him more than it needs anything else.

The church was born of the Spirit, in Acts 2, at Pentecost. The Spirit had been *with* the disciples before then, but he was not *in* them and they were not *in* him.

At Pentecost, Jesus baptised the church in the Holy Spirit; and, since then, the church has always had access to him and to his power.

After Pentecost, the disciples had to learn to live in the Spirit, to pray in the Spirit, to walk with the Spirit, to depend on the Spirit, to be guided by the Spirit – and so on. It is impossible to imagine the New Testament church apart from the Spirit: without him, there may be an organisation, but there can never be a church.

THE HOLY SPIRIT

The Holy Spirit is fully personal and fully God – and we examine the biblical teaching about him in *Knowing the Spirit*. He is always the Holy Spirit, or the Spirit of God, or the Spirit of Christ; he is never 'the Spirit of the church'.

The church is meant to be filled by him, but no church possesses or controls him. Instead, he wants to fill the church, to possess us, to teach us, to guide us, to empower us, to transform us, and to work in partnership with us.

We cannot confine him

The church can neither control nor confine the Spirit. We cannot insist that he works in a certain way or through specific ceremonies, words or offices. The Scriptures do offer clear promises, conditions and principles about the Spirit – but they also make it plain that 'the wind or breath of God' blows where he wills.

Every expression of the church must learn to listen to the Spirit, to hear what he is saying to the churches, and to obey him. Our traditions must always bow to him, as he seeks constantly to renew us and lead us onwards to our glorious destiny.

We do not monopolise him

No expression of the church can claim that they have a special relationship with the Spirit. All believers have the Spirit within them, so no one group can have a monopoly of him.

Some believers may be filled with the Spirit, but this filling is available to *all* believers. There is no special relationship of the Spirit which is open to some parts of the church and closed to others.

The helper

In John 14:16–18, Jesus promised to send the Spirit to the church as the *parakletos*: this means 'called alongside' and can be translated as 'helper', 'encourager', 'comforter', 'counsellor' or 'advocate'. He is the church's helper.

John 14:16–18 ☐

It is vitally important that we depend on his help, as we can do nothing in the realm of the Spirit without him.

We cannot function effectively in any area of church life without his help. All our activities are meaningless and empty without him.

For example, without his help we cannot:

- *worship* – John 4:24

John 4:24 ☐

- *witness* – Acts 1:8

Acts 1:8 ☐

- *minister* – 1 Corinthians 12:4–11

1 Corinthians 12:4–11 ☐

- *pray* – Ephesians 6:18; Romans 8:26

Ephesians 6:18 ☐

Romans 8:26 ☐

- *be guided* – Romans 8:14

8:14 ☐

- *defeat the enemy* – Matthew 12:28; Ephesians 3:6

Matthew 12:28 ☐

Ephesians 3:6 ☐

- *learn* – John 14:26; 16:13

John 14:26 ☐

16:13 ☐

The teacher

In John 14:17 & 16:13, Jesus promised that the Spirit of truth would guide us into all truth – and that he would glorify Jesus – by taking the things of Jesus and declaring them to us. He is the church's teacher.

The Spirit does not go *beyond* Jesus' words, and he does not lead us into *new* truth. Instead he teaches us from Jesus' inexhaustible revelation and leads us into *all* truth.

The Spirit does not say more than Jesus, instead he reminds us of what Jesus has said – John 14:26; 15:15. He often helps us, however, to see what Jesus has revealed in a new light or fresh way.

John 14:26 ☐

15:15 ☐

This *Sword of the Spirit* series is sub-titled 'a school of ministry in the Word and the Spirit' because there is a tremendously close link between the Word and the Spirit. The Spirit is bound to the eternal Word of God – which 2 Timothy 3:16 shows he inspired or out-breathed. But the Spirit is not confined to the Scriptures, for he speaks to us in many different ways. What he says, however, is always consistent with the scriptural revelation.

2 Timothy 3:16 ☐

We need his help to understand the Word, but we cannot hold all truth in perfect balance – God's word is simply too vast and our understanding too imperfect. This means that our teacher is constantly giving us fresh insights into certain aspects of the truth which we have forgotten or neglected, and which are particularly relevant for our situation.

The witness

John 15:26 ☐
16:14 ☐

In John 15:26, Jesus taught that the Spirit would bear witness to Jesus. He is 'the witness'. In fact, everything that he does is done with the single purpose of glorifying Jesus – John 16:14.

He comes alongside and helps the church, so that we will glorify Jesus; he leads us into all truth – so that we will glorify Jesus; he guides and empowers us – so that we will glorify Jesus, and so on.

When he came upon the church at Pentecost, it was essentially to equip and empower the disciples as effective witnesses. He also filled them with joy and forged them into a caring fellowship, but – primarily – he filled them with his power for mission and witness.

Any experience of the Spirit which does not result in more effective witness to Jesus has to be questioned. He wants the church to open itself to him so that he can sweep away our fears and embarrassment, and fill us with his boldness and words. Witness to Jesus is so important to the Spirit that he provides us with both the power to speak and the words to say.

The Spirit's primary concern is that God's people, Christ's body, should get on with its divinely-ordained job of taking the gospel to all nations. If we have an ounce of compassion for the people around us, and a scrap of zeal for the glory of God, we will throw ourselves upon the Spirit and ask him to help us be ever more effective witnesses to our risen Lord.

The giver

1 Corinthians 12 teaches that the Spirit is a great giver of gifts to the church, and verses 7–11 lists some of the gifts that he keeps on giving.

1 Corinthians 14 shows that these gifts are given to build the church up and to help it function more effectively. If we are serious about the church, we really will be zealous for the gifts.

But 1 Corinthians 13 suggests that love is even more important than the gifts. 1 Corinthians 14:1 makes it plain that we should not chose between gifts and love, for we are called to pursue and to desire both – but love must be pre-eminent.

The church of Christ is meant to be a great missionary community, it is meant to be a strong guardian of the Word, it is meant to be an effective fighting force – but it is nothing without love. In fact, we can say that the quality of a church's loving is the measure of their spiritual renewal and maturity, not the quantity of their gifts or the volume of their activities.

As we open ourselves up to the Spirit, so his love for the Father and the Son fill and control us. Ephesians 3:17 promises that the church will be rooted and grounded in love and that we will know the love of Christ which passes knowledge. This is our destiny in the church.

And, as we are changed by the Spirit, so we begin to love each other with his love. Ephesians 4:25–32 & 1 Thessalonians 5:19–22 show that he is grieved and quenched by our lack of love. 1 John 4:20 is even more striking. This shows that the Spirit yearns for the church to be characterised by God's self-sacrificing love.

THE SPIRIT LEADS US TO MATURITY

When we walk in and with the Spirit, we can be sure that he will lead us on to the church's glorious destiny which is set out in Ephesians 4.

The Spirit will complete what he began at Pentecost. He will establish an effective, functioning church so that a mature bride is ready when Jesus returns. Jesus promised that he would build his church, and Ephesians 4 shows that the building will be completed.

1 Corinthians
12:7–11 ☐
14:1 ☐

Ephesians 3:17 ☐

Ephesians
4:25–32 ☐

1 Thessalonians
5:19–22 ☐

1 John 4:20 ☐

As Christ's body, the church is God's representative in the world. Christ's work on earth can only be carried out through his body. When it is not a mature, strong and healthy body, the work of Christ is not done. But when the body is strong, and growing towards maturity, God's work on earth can be accomplished.

Ephesians
4:11–16 ☐
1:23 ☐

Ephesians 4:11–16 describes the church attaining the fullness of Christ. This means that, one day, the church will perfectly reveal Christ in all his fullness *on earth*. This underlines Ephesians 1:23, where the church is described as 'the fullness of him'.

Jesus has given apostles, prophets, evangelists, pastors and teachers to his church to knit God's people *together* for the work of service. It is this which builds up Christ's body, and these leaders are meant to go on with their work, building up the church, until four things occur.

1.   Unity

The church will reach the unity of the faith. This is not the unity of the Spirit which began at the cross and already exists, but unity in the essential doctrines of the faith and a mature understanding of Christ.

This does not mean that all Christians will believe exactly the same things about everything, but rather that there will be strong unity in all the essentials of the faith throughout the whole church.

2.   Full knowledge

The mature church will reach a full knowledge of the Son of God. This is not an improved version of our knowledge; it is *full* knowledge.

Philippians
3:8–16 ☐
2:5–11 ☐

In Philippians 3:8–16, Paul longs to know Christ, and the power of his resurrection, and the depth of his sufferings. And in Philippians 2:5–11, he urges us to make the mind of Christ our own. He offers a roller-coaster description of the Son of God who emptied himself, took the form of a slave, accepted death, and was raised so high that all beings everywhere should bend the knee to him.

The church begins to rise towards this full knowledge of the Son when it moves beyond wanting power for its own sake, and longs to think and be like Jesus – when we yearn to share his power *and* his suffering. We can be sure that, sometime soon, we will experience this full reality in every area of church life.

3.   Full stature

The mature church will form the perfect human; we will be of full stature, fully mature. We will no longer be children, tossed one way or another; instead we will be strong and mature in Christ. Despite what some people say, the church is not dying out; it is not fading away – it is coming of age.

The church we read about in the New Testament is the infant church. The end-time church will be a mature, adult, vigorous church. If the early church was able to achieve so much, what will the end-time church accomplish?

If the biblical promises mean anything, we can surely expect that the coming biblical church will experience a massive outpouring of the Spirit which will lead to effective world-wide evangelism. We will take the gospel to all nations. God's glory will be seen throughout the earth. There will be glory in the church by Christ Jesus.

4.   Christ's fullness

Ephesians 4:13 follows on from Ephesians 1:22–23 to show that the mature church will be filled with the fullness of Christ himself. This means we will be so full of Jesus that we can accurately represent him in the world – genuinely reveal his glory – and achieve everything he has asked.

Ephesians
1:22–23 ☐

This biblical, mature church will be full of his power, his wisdom, his love and his authority. It will show the world the fullness of his grace and holiness. The glory of God will be fully manifest both in us and though us.

The Christ-full church will be a body of credible, active witnesses throughout the entire world, in every nation and culture. This is surely a vision worth working and praying towards, a dream worth living and dying for. Even the smallest step towards it will be extremely valuable.

As we live by the truth and in love, we will grow completely into Christ – who is the head by whom the whole body is fitted and joined together. Every joint will add its own strength for each individual part to work according to its function. So the church will keep on growing, until it has been fully and finally built in love.

ACTIVITIES for individuals and small groups

the glory of god

If you were to ask a group of people in your church, 'What are the purposes of our church?' what sort of answers do you imagine they would give?

....

....

....

....

What is God's single main aim for your church?

....

....

How can you align people's purposes for your church more closely with God's purpose?

....

....

....

....

When was God's glory usually seen in the Old Testament?

....

....

....

What does 'glory' really mean?

....

....

What is your experience of God's glory?

....

....

....

....

1.   *How can you personally experience more of God's glory?*

....

....

....

....

....

2.   *How can you reveal more of God's glory?*

....

....

....

....

....

Which of these two questions is more important? Why is this?

....

....

....

If self-sacrifice is the secret of fruitfulness:

How, practically, can you apply this principle in your life?

....

....

....

....

How, practically, can your church apply this principle?

....

....

....

....

the church of christ

What does Matthew 16:18 teach about the church?

....

....

....

How does this passage show that the church should be characterised by a warlike nature?

....

....

How, practically, is your church troubling the gates of Hades?

....

....

....

John 17 reveals the longings in Jesus' heart just before his death, and offers a panoramic view of God's purposes for the church on earth. Although John 17 does not specifically refer to 'the church', it is plain that this is Jesus' intercession for his church.

Read John 17 carefully in several different translations. What does this chapter teach about glory and the church?

....

....

....

....

What are the implications of this for your church?

....

....

....

....

How are you guarding the Word of God?

....

....

How should your church use the Word of God in mission?

....

....

....

....

What is the relationship between joy and grace?

....

....

What, practically, does it mean for a church to be filled with joy?

....

....

....

How is your church maintaining the oneness of the church with other expressions of the church in your locality?

....

....

....

Read John 17 again. What does it teach us about the church and the world?

....

....

....

....

How is your church involved in and with the world?

....

....

....

the gathering

What does ekklesia *mean?*

....

....

How is this related to the Holy Spirit?

....

....

What can your church learn from the Greek background to ekklesia*?*

....

....

The gathered people of God in the Old Testament – the congregation, assembly, company of Israel – teach four principle truths about the church.

How was Israel gathered from the world?

....

....

How does this 'foreshadow' the church?

....

....

....

How was Israel gathered together?

....

....

What does this imply for your church?

....

....

....

How was Israel gathered for a relationship?

....

....

What relationships have you been gathered for?

....

....

What was the destiny that Israel was gathered for?

....

....

What is the purpose behind our gathering in the church?

....

....

....

Who is included in the universal church?

....

....

What is your 'local' – in the New Testament sense – church?

....

....

Which is your 'household' church?

....

....

How can you ensure that buildings and meetings do not control your church life?

....

....

....

....

....

the fellowship

What does the word koinonia *teach about the life of the church?*

....
....
....

What are the requirements for scriptural fellowship?

....
....
....
....

How, practically, have you experienced fellowship in the last three months?

....
....
....
....
....

Why is giving so deeply involved in New Testament fellowship?

....
....
....

How can your church develop the giving element of fellowship?

....
....
....
....
....
....

Koinonia includes *everything* that we are called to do together as Christians. Fellowship can be expressed in obvious ways like prayer, worship, social activities and practical work; but the New Testament highlights five main ways that the church should express fellowship.

How can the way your church celebrates communion be developed to enhance fellowship?

....

....

....

....

....

How, practically, can you develop fellowship with financially needy Christians?

....

....

....

How do you choose the Christian ministries that you support?

....

....

....

Who have you recently supported in suffering? How did you fellowship with them?

....

....

....

....

....

What is God saying to you about fellowship?

....

....

....

....

....

pictures of the church

What three principles about the church are implied in every biblical picture of the church?

....

....

....

Why are we God's people?

....

....

....

....

How, practically, can you develop a greater awareness of the church's corporate nature?

....

....

....

....

What are the practical implications for your church of being part of the one body of Christ in your area?

....

....

....

....

What divides you from some parts of the body?

....

....

....

....

What is God saying to you about divisions within the body?

....

....

....

....

Why did God choose a tabernacle-type building for Israel?

....

....

....

....

Why do most people usually prefer a temple-type building for their churches?

....

....

....

....

What practical preparations should your church be making for becoming part of the bride of Christ?

....

....

....

....

Which picture of the church do you find most helpful and comforting? Why is this?

....

....

....

Which picture do you find most disturbing? Why is this?

....

....

....

the church and the kingdom

What is the kingdom of God?

....

....

What are the differences between the kingdom and the church?

....

....

....

Which is more important, to extend God's kingdom in your area, or to increase the size of your church?

....

....

What would happen in your church if revival broke out in a neighbouring church from a different tradition?

....

....

....

How should 'kingdom thinking' affect the content and purpose of our witnessing and mission?

....

....

....

....

....

What is the relationship between Israel and the church?

....

....

....

What should our attitude be to the conflict between Israel and the Arab nations?

....

....

....

How should we pray for Israel?

....

....

How can we most helpfully remember and celebrate the essential Jewish tree into which we have been grafted?

....

....

....

What does Jesus' answer in Matthew 22:15–22 teach?

....

....

....

In any controversial situation, what would be legitimate prophetic proclamation and 'salt' influence, and what would be illegitimate attempts to impose God's rule?

....

....

....

....

....

How, practically, has your church's attitude to the state affected your church's activities?

....

....

....

....

....

belonging to the church

In your church, which of the four basic steps of Christian initiation is least emphasised? Why is this?

....

....

....

How should the four steps of initiation affect our witness and mission?

....

....

....

When you became a Christian, what changes did you have to make in your thinking?

....

....

....

What have you 'changed your mind' about in the last few months?

....

....

....

When you received the Spirit, what changes did you experience in your life?

....

....

....

How has the Spirit affected your life in the last few weeks?

....

....

....

How do people in your church know that you are committed to them?

....

....

....

What is your experience of spiritual companionship?

....

....

....

How can this be developed in your life?

....

....

....

How can your church cell groups become more effective caring and training groups?

....

....

....

Which of the five expressions of church do you find most helpful? Why is this?

....

....

....

Which of them are you least comfortable in? Why is this?

....

....

....

What changes do you need to make to have better balance of church commitment?

....

....

....

leadership in the church

What are the three basic biblical principles of church structure?

....

....

....

Which of these principles is least evident in your church?

....

....

How can this be remedied?

....

....

....

....

What is the system of leadership in your church?

....

What are the strengths and weaknesses of this system as it works in your church?

....

....

....

....

What are the biblical differences between a bishop and an elder?

....

....

What is the biblical basis for having a single elder/bishop/leader in a local church?

....

....

How do you support your local leaders?

....

....

....

What qualities should we look for in local church leaders?

....

....

....

Which of these qualities is least evident in your life?

....

....

Why is this? How can it change?

....

....

....

....

....

What is the primary function of all the trans-local leaders in Ephesians 4:11?

....

....

In what aspects of leadership has God gifted you?

....

....

How should you be developing your leadership gifts?

....

....

....

....

the functioning church

What does worship really mean?

....

....

List all the different ways that you have worshipped God in the last week.

....

....

....

....

....

What cultural and traditional factors influence your church's worship?

....

....

....

....

Which of these factors is sometimes confused with worship 'in the Spirit'?

....

....

How do you build up the body of Christ by your worship?

....

....

....

Which of your church's traditions conflict with the Scriptures?

....

....

....

How are you studying the Scriptures?

....
....
....
....

Which parts of the Bible do you study least frequently? Why is this?

....
....
....
....

What is the most important truth that you have learnt from the Bible in the last three months?

....
....
....

Whom are you witnessing to at the moment?

....

How are you witnessing to them?

....
....
....

Whom is your church focusing on witnessing to this year?

....
....

How are you reaching them?

....
....
....
....

What are the strengths and weaknesses of pastoral care in your church?

....
....
....
....
....
....

How, practically, could you contribute more to caring for other people in your church?

....
....
....
....

What pastoral care do you need?

....
....
....
....

What are you and your church contributing to community care?

....
....
....

Please read Acts 2:40–47 & 4:31–37. How is the early church functioning in worship, witness, word and welfare?

....
....
....
....
....
....

the sacraments of the church

What is a sacrament?

....
....
....

In what ways are baptism and communion signs of God's grace?

....
....
....

How does God use baptism and communion to underline the fact that he wants a relationship with us, a partnership in and with the Spirit?

....
....
....

What does 'baptism' mean?

....
....

Please read these passages and note what is associated with baptism.

John 3:5; Acts 2:38, 41–47; 22:16; Romans 6:1–14; 1 Corinthians 6:11; 12:13; Galatians 3:26–29; Colossians 2:11–3:17; Titus 3:5–6.

....
....
....
....
....
....
....

If you have been baptised, what did God pledge to you through baptism?

....

....

....

....

How have these pledges been fulfilled in your experience?

....

....

....

....

If you have not been baptised, why have you not taken this step?

....

....

....

How do you prepare yourself for communion?

....

....

....

What does God do for you in and through communion?

....

....

....

How, practically, could your church make its celebration of communion more central, relevant and meaningful?

....

....

....

....

....

the spirit and the church

What does your church need more than anything else?

....

What are you doing to ensure that your church receives this?

....

....

....

With which of your Christian activities could you continue without the Holy Spirit?

....

....

....

How has the Holy Spirit helped you in the last month?

....

....

....

....

....

How do you expect your church to change in the next year?

....

....

....

What is the God's present purpose for your church?

....

....

....

....

What is God's ultimate destiny for your church?

....

....

....

Please read Ephesians 4:11–16, using several different versions of the Bible. Ask God to speak you from these verses about your church situation.

Which verse, or part of a verse, is most important for your situation? Why is this?

....

....

....

What is God asking you to do to ensure that verses 13–16 are fulfilled in the life and experience of your church?

....

....

....

....

What is the most important principle that you have learnt about the church?

....

....

....

What is God asking you to believe?

....

....

....

What is God asking you to do?

....

....

....